THE **STORY** OF **BRUTUS**

THE **STORY** OF **BRUTUS**

MY LIFE WITH BRUTUS THE BEAR
AND THE GRIZZLIES OF NORTH AMERICA

CASEY ANDERSON

PEGASUS BOOKS
NEW YORK

THE STORY OF BRUTUS

Pegasus Books LLC
80 Broad Street, 5th Floor
New York, NY 10004

Copyright © 2010 by Casey Anderson

First Pegasus Books cloth edition September 2010

Interior design by Maria Fernandez

ISBN: 978-1-60598-253-3

10 9 8 7 8 6 5 4 3 2 1

Printed in the United States of America
Distributed by W. W. Norton & Company, Inc.

DEDICATION

Wᴴᴱɴ ɪ ꜱᴀᴛ ᴅᴏᴡɴ ᴛᴏ ᴡʀɪᴛᴇ ᴛʜɪꜱ ʙᴏᴏᴋ, ɪᴛ ᴡᴀꜱ ʟɪᴋᴇ opening a treasure chest of memories. As I dug deep into my mind, I often relived and felt each moment and remembered the forgotten. What a wild ride it has been since the very beginning. But along the way, one thing stood out to me very clearly. I was born with a passion, a desire to pursue a career and lifestyle that was very unorthodox and outside the box, so to speak. Without the full support of my family and friends, I would never be where I am now. Most people would call me crazy and ask me why I didn't I go get a real job. I never had that obstacle. I was allowed to run free and follow my dreams, and was often encouraged, even when there seemed to be little hope. My father, mother, brothers, and sister all stood by my decisions and put their fear aside, knowing that I was living the life I wanted. Others believed in my dreams and came along for the ride, dedicating their own lives and allowing the dream to continue. Dad, Mom & Tim, Jeremy, Patrick, Aaron, Windy, and the rest of my family, thank you for being my foundation. John, Ami, Judy, and my Montana Grizzly Encounter crew, thank you for being my strong and nurturing heart, pumping relentlessly and keeping our dream alive. Thank you to the Grizzly Creek Film team for helping take this dream to another level. And to my beautiful wife Missi, thank you for being my soul mate, giving me inspiration, and being my hero. Without you, I would be lost in the wilderness of loneliness. I write this book for all who remain untamed as they follow their hearts, and of course, for my best friend, Brutus.

CONTENTS

LETTER FROM THE EDITOR

Wₕₑₙ I FIRST "DISCOVERED" CASEY AND HIS REMARKABLE relationship with Brutus, stories like "Christian the Lion" and Tarra the elephant and her best friend, Bella, a dog, had already charmed millions, as I myself had been. I was always hoping that I too would have the chance to be part of a story that touched so many.

My own journey into bear country began with a photo of Brutus sharing a Thanksgiving "turkey" with Casey Anderson and his family in Montana, and soon segued into a visit to the National Geographic website and clips of Anderson's show, "Expedition Grizzly" and "Expedition Wild," Brutus's very own web page, and the remarkable organization that is the Montana Grizzly Encounter.

What struck me at once about Anderson and Brutus was that, for all the other heartwarming animal stories out there, theirs alone focused on conservation, education, and protecting the integrity of our natural world. Not content with being a YouTube phenomenon, Casey took it upon himself many years ago to create a preserve to foster bears like

Brutus who had been born into captivity (in some cases, cruel and inhuman captivity) and could not be returned to the wild, yet who still deserved to grow up and live out their lives "being bears." This preserve would also be a way for people to see grizzlies in a more natural state and learn about these magnificent, powerful creatures, who are neither bloodthirsty killers nor giant teddy bears. They are complex, emotional creatures who form lifelong relationships and truly have the capacity to love. Cubs will cry when their mother abandons them; Brutus jokes with Casey and loves to ham it up for company as much as any budding Hollywood starlet. He has his own personality, distinct from other bears out there, as they too have their own unique temperaments and characters.

But an even more important facet of Casey and Brutus's work is educating us humans, the adaptive species, on how we can better live alongside our grizzly neighbors. Bears and humans have always had a close bond: the sloth bears in India, the spectacled bears of Peru, the polar bear paparazzi in Canada. Yet this relationship has become strained in recent years, and it is up to us to make it right. And there is no place better to start than in one of the greatest bear enclaves in the world, Yellowstone National Park.

As someone who has been fascinated by the natural world since childhood and a staunch advocate for environmental protection, I found this part of Casey's mission to be the most compelling of all, prompting me to pick up the phone almost two years ago and contact the Encounter. This was a story that needed to reach a wider audience so that even city slickers like me can understand the fascinating nuances of animal behavior and experience the wonders of an icy cold night on a mountainside, with only grizzlies and moths for company. This story needed to be told so that recreational backpackers can understand the world they are entering when they step out onto the trail—so that the braided path of bear and human existence will continue for a new generation. Never before has the bond between man and bear been so intimately explored, and I hope you will be as moved by the remarkable *Story of Brutus* as I was.

Jessica Case
Pegasus Books
New York, 2010

THE STORY OF BRUTUS

CHAPTER 1
COCO AND CORKY

THERE IS NOTHING SPECIAL ABOUT ME, BUT BRUTUS IS
an exceptional grizzly bear, who just happens to have me for
a pet.

Brutus came into the world as any grizzly cub would, but
it was clear from day one that this bear was special. I was
twenty-six years old, and I had been working with animals
professionally in some respect for about eight years and was
now a curator at a drive-through wildlife park in Idaho.
Brutus was born in a small man-made cave we had constructed of concrete and steel to give the cubs the feel of
being born into a real "cave." Our replication wasn't perfect,
but it sheltered the tiny newborns from the brutal eastern

Idaho winter weather. Brutus clung close to his mother for warmth and nourishment, and acknowledged the clues of the mysterious world that awaited him. Along with the howls of the January winds, he could also hear the rumble of a Chevy engine, and the muffled voices of his future—humans. Most grizzly bear cubs would learn to fear these sounds, but Brutus was developing what would become a curious love affair and affinity with them, since his mother, who had been in captivity her entire life, perked up to our presence and did not react in fear.

One cold, clear February day, Brutus's life changed in an instant. If cubs are not removed at a very young age, they cannot be handled, and come early spring, male bears will kill them in order to mate with the female. Female bears defend their cubs fiercely, even if they are used to humans, so to prevent our being mauled by a defensive mother, we would immobilize her to remove the cubs. He was pinned beneath the weight of his tranquilized 400-pound mother. As he squirmed, he was suddenly freed as I rolled his mom to the side with a labored heave, and I scooped up what was going to become my son into my arms and sheltered him from the crisp winter air. He let out a little cry, and like a new father I held him closer and looked into his little brown eyes with paternal pride but also with the newfound fear that all new parents have of the unknown days that are to come.

His first moments of the new world were bittersweet. I tried to imagine the overwhelming rush that must have flooded his senses. He seemed to be uncomfortable and scared for the first time, but then he nestled his head into mine and found a new calmness. So the bond of trust was born. He sheltered his little wet nose in the bristly hairs of my goatee. It wasn't Mom's soft, silver-tipped fur, but the coarse brown hair must have felt good. Little did he know at that point that he would be greatly responsible for turning my brown hair silver-tipped, too. My warm and loving arms would soon be etched with little bloody grizzly bear scratches and painted with mustard-colored cub diarrhea. But those battles were to come. Meanwhile, the connection that would form between two species that usually are segregated by fear would be life-changing. Brutus never had the opportunity to become prejudiced against humans, a behavior that is learned, not instinctual. In fact, in a staggering way, his heartstrings were tugged in the opposite direction.

BEFORE BRUTUS CAME ALONG, I HAD GOTTEN TO KNOW HIS parents quite well. His father was Corky and his mother was Coco. Both of them had been owned by a woman who trained bears for the television and film industry. Coco seemed much more amenable to training than Corky. In fact, rumor had it that Corky had been put to the side and ignored a bit because the other bears he lived with were used more often for movie jobs, but the result was an attention-yearning sweetheart. Corky was very charming, very peaceful, and just plain laid-back. As far as grizzly bears go, he was perfect, and didn't seem to miss the proverbial spotlight one little bit. On the other hand, Coco was spunky and full of life. Corky and Coco spent their time together in their very own enclosure at the wildlife park. Coco was the boss, even though she was only about half the size of Corky. Not that different from some human couples in that respect!

Coco and Corky's enclosure was separated by two 5-foot-tall electric fences that paralleled one another approximately 10 feet apart. Just on the other side was the enclosure where approximately thirty black bears lived. One of my favorite memories was of the mating season. Two female black bears, Rosie and Hannah, would walk to the fence's edge and flirt with Corky, admiring his big, beautiful male grizzly stature. Corky loved the attention and would hover just on the other side and show off by digging massive holes, pushing over trees, and standing on his hind legs, showing those black-bear ladies that he was much more than just your average bear. But Corky was not the only one with an interspecies admirer. A large male black bear named Leonard would also walk the fence's edge and flirt with Coco. She was not as impressed, but I did see her give some signs of interest, enough to keep Leonard around—the tease!

Though Corky was ten years old when I first met him, anytime I was near him he would engage me with full-on eye contact. I could tell that he desperately wanted to interact. From all that I'd learned up until that moment, interacting with a ten-year-old grizzly bear for the very first time would be foolish. But something was different about Corky. So despite the rules, the owner's wishes, and to the chagrin of my fellow keepers, every day after work I would sneak down alone into the grizzly enclosure and spend some time with Corky. I started off with baby steps. I would feed him by hand over the safety of the fence to build his trust. Gradually, as he became more relaxed, I would touch his face with the hand I wasn't using to feed him. He would turn to smell the new hand but would go back to the food. Then, it moved to food-free touching. This allowed him to concentrate on me and investigate me a bit more. I then moved to crossing the fence and standing next to him, again with food to build a trust. Then, when the food was removed, this was the biggest step because it was just the two of us, without barriers, standing together exploring each other. I would have to swallow my fear or apprehension so as not to introduce the element of anxiety to the newfound bond. I continued in this fashion, little by little, until one night, I got to the point I could sit in his lap. In a process like this, you learn so much about communication with a grizzly bear. Each moment has to be analyzed very carefully, and any misinterpretations would end badly. If I had walked into a situation like this with too much or too little confidence, I would have been destroyed. Finding a balance, creating respect, and crossing the lines only when invited are special skills that I feel we all have. The hard part is just digging them out from beneath all the clutter and trash of our uncharitable minds.

It didn't take long for Corky and me to develop a close bond, a bond that I had to show off. Nobody could believe it, and although they had been opposed to my starting this relationship, everybody was astonished. The relationship became so close that I could sit on Corky's lap as he nuzzled my face and I scratched his belly. There was something in his eyes and in his gentle mannerisms that invited me in. I had worked with perhaps fifty adult bears, and I'd never taken a leap of faith the way I did with Corky. It was ironic that I had picked the biggest grizzly bear I had ever worked with to be my first for such a relationship.

Coco, on the other hand, was much harder to control. I

often thought that Coco was too smart for her own good. I would watch her watch Corky and me. She would pay special attention to our patterns. Something about her kept me on my toes. She would show off her tricks without being asked and engage you in a way to draw you in closer. Then, just when you let your guard down and were close enough, she would take a swipe at you. If she wasn't going to be the bear getting all the attention at the park, then she was going to make the headlines for ripping your face off.

One morning, I woke early to the ringing of my cell phone. I lived on the premises of the wildlife park in a small trailer at the time. On the phone was my boss. He said, "Casey, I just got a call from the Sheriff's Department and they said there is a grizzly bear on the highway!" That was the worst news in the world to wake up to in those days. I leapt up from my bed, threw on my clothes, and called my partner, Christine, for backup. I drove into the wildlife park, looking for a bear on all sides. I did not see anything on the highway, and the traffic wasn't reacting as if there was a grizzly on the road. As I drove near the grizzly enclosure, I'll never forget what I saw: a large pile of freshly excavated dirt and a tunnel going underneath the gate. On the other side sat Corky with a confused look. I remember thinking that of the two grizzly bears who could have escaped, I was hoping it was Corky. He would have been the easier of the two to get back into the grizzly enclosure. Coco, on the other hand, would have created a ruckus if we had to do anything with her. I looked back toward the corner of the large elk, deer, and bison enclosure, and I noticed that all of the hooved animals were paying close attention to something or someone. Just then, Christine rounded the corner in her little white jeep.

Christine had previously worked with most of the bears now in the wildlife park. She hadn't had very much experience with Coco, but it was certainly more than I had had. Coco, who had now escaped through the tunnel and was having second thoughts, sat terrified on the edge of the ungulate enclosure. Christine and I came up with a game plan. Christine was going to walk alongside Coco and lead her back to the gate with treats. It was our hope that once we got her back to the gate, in fear of her new surroundings, she would willingly return to the comforts of her own enclosure. We walked along with Coco, marshmallow by marshmallow, leading her step-by-step slowly toward her escape route.

About halfway across the 30-acre enclosure, Coco started to get nervous and began to hesitate. Some of the occupants of the enclosure, a large flock of wild turkeys, were making their way over to see their new friend. Coco did not want to be friends with the wild turkeys. In fact, she seemed to be scared of them. Coco sat down in the middle of the road that wound through the enclosure. She began sucking on Christine's finger, a sign of nervousness, but was finding some pacification in the sucking. Christine and I spoke to each other in a calm way and came up with plan B.

Christine was going to stand there allowing Coco to continue to suck on her finger while I returned to the truck and got the makings of a small electrical fence. I was going to come back and put the fence up around her to contain her and then we would go and get the bear trailer and attempt to load her into it. I went back to the truck, gathered up the items, and slowly returned to Christine. I was about 20 yards away when it happened. With lightning speed, Christine was engulfed in a barrage of brutal strikes and bites from Coco. Christine collapsed to the ground, and Coco sprinted away in full panic.

I ran to Christine and noticed that she was beginning to go into some sort of shock. I gave her a once-over and, not seeing any obvious wounds, scooped her into my arms and carried her to the truck. I remember asking her if she was okay, and by her reaction I knew she wasn't. I began to look closely at her and noticed blood soaking through her sweatshirt. I pulled back her sleeve. It was bad. Most of her arm on either side of her elbow looked like hamburger meat. I kept my cool, trying not to let her see the panic welling up inside me. I quickly drove her out of the park and rendezvoused with one of the park owners. I asked him to rush her to the emergency room while I returned to attempt to contain and extinguish the emergency situation that had been left behind.

Christine went off to the hospital and I returned to Coco.* I wasn't messing around now, and three tranquilizer darts later I dragged Coco's unconscious body back into her enclosure. Corky, who was sitting there watching the whole event, gave us both curious looks as if he wondered what all the fuss was about. The park staff decided to keep Coco around. She was a spitfire, but she was the only breeding female grizzly bear they had. Grizzly bear cubs were a vital asset in order to attract visitors to the park, so despite her disposition and rap

---

* Christine recovered from her injuries. She now lives happily with her family in Minnesota, but no longer works with bears.

sheet, they decided to let her stay. (Her enclosure was fortified to be escape proof.)

I find it a general rule of thumb that female grizzlies tend
to be a little more moody than their male counterparts. I
speculate that it comes from their relentless protection of
their cubs. Whether protecting them from humans, other
bears, or countless other obstacles, they must always be on
guard, and they almost always choose an offensive strategy if
they sense danger. As I got to know Brutus over the years, I
saw equal parts of his father and mother in him. Brutus will
always be 100 percent a grizzly bear, and I never forget that
50 percent of that is Coco.

CHAPTER 2

HYBRID

I WAS BORN IN MONTANA. MY DAD WAS A MOUNTAIN MAN AND my mom ran a homeless shelter. Now I give homeless grizzly bears a place to live. My mother's side of the family have been cattle ranchers in Montana for several generations, and politically conservative, while my father's family were mostly fairly liberal, so I got a healthy dose of different opinions while I was growing up. I would like to think it expanded my mind and gave me a chance to understand both sides of an issue, although as it usually is between parents and children, there were some bumps along the way.

When my father had any free time, it was spent in the mountains, and I was hot on his heels. Whether it was gathering firewood, hunting, hiking, or camping, most of my childhood was spent exploring the surrounding forests. My dad believed in wilderness and liked the land to be pure and untouched. He would complain about motorcycles and clear-cut logging, and if we encountered on public land the type of barbed wire fence used for cattle, we usually destroyed it. I was an ecoterrorist in training, and some of those ideals still run deep in my soul. Ironically, the next weekend, we could be found at my mom's family's cattle ranch fixing fences, riding around on four-wheelers to check the calves, and talking about falling cattle prices and the potential of selling agricultural land to subdivision developers.

Growing up in Montana was wonderful, but being raised in a family with a dichotomy of perception about wilderness was confusing. However, it did give me a wide perspective, and one thing both sides had in common was the love for animals. It is here, at my roots, that the obvious need to coexist with the wilderness became a seed that I have been cultivating my entire life.

I love both sides of my family, and I have watched them adjust to each other over the years. They have found some sort of harmony and respect in each other's opinions, and they have listened and adapted accordingly, and I think it is time for the rest of the world to do the same.

My mother directed a homeless shelter in Helena, Montana, for most of my childhood. The shelter took in mostly homeless men, whose background ranged from Vietnam vets to the mentally ill. My mother instilled many values in me, but the one that sticks with me in my interactions with wild animals—and people, too—is the value of *never* judging a book by its cover.

Many of the men my mother helped and cared for are the same people that many will take one look at and step back from. Our closed minds have made us cower from them as if they have leprosy or are going to steal something from us. My mother made friends with these people, and so did I. It didn't take me long to realize how very wrong the common perception of most transient people is. The people I met were caring, honest, and intelligent. My mother met some of her closest friends at the shelter. Those friends continue to be some of her most loyal. I learned a lot from my mother when it came to blind compassion, and sacrificing your own comfort for the comfort of others. There is no greater gift than to take your favorite shirt off your back and give it to someone who needs it more than you. This is the basis of my passion to help grizzly bears and other wild creatures. Like the homeless men and women on the streets across the country, grizzly bears are misjudged and treated poorly out of fear and ignorance. Mom taught me to learn about and understand them.

Transient people are often identified by nicknames. "Canada" was a grizzly-bear-sized man who had ridden the rails from north of the border in Ontario to Montana to start a new life. He was a gentle giant. Though he was a massive, hairy man who would have intimidated most people, he was as soft-hearted as a lamb and as loyal as a person could be. We would talk about the wilds of the north, and he would encourage me to chase my dreams to work with wildlife. Not too long after, when my dreams began to take shape, I started working at Yellowstone Bear World as the curator. I wanted two weeks off to go scuba diving in Cozumel, Mexico, but it was the height of the tourist season at the park, and the park's owner did not want to be left short-handed during this valuable time, so he made me a deal. If I could find someone experienced with grizzly bears to fill in for me during those two weeks, he would allow me to go. I didn't know anyone with that kind of experience. My tropical plans were certainly doomed.

That night Canada's name popped into my head. Though he had absolutely no grizzly bear experience—in fact, his only experience with animals was maybe petting a stray cocker spaniel—I knew he would do anything for me. I called the homeless shelter in Helena and got him on the phone. I explained the situation, and we fabricated a plan. We came up with a story that would fool my boss. Canada was going to pose as a guy who used to be a zookeeper at some wildlife park in Ontario that we found on the Internet. He was going to say he had just moved to the United States to look for work, and I happened to find him at this opportune time. We laughed as we created this far-fetched story, but I could sense his apprehension to be thrown to the bears, so to speak. Our next dilemma was getting him from Montana to Idaho. He didn't have a car, and I didn't have time to drive up and get him. Canada decided to travel the way he knew best, and that was by freight train. He mapped out the routes, and figured he would be in Pocatello, Idaho, sometime between 10 a.m. and 4 p.m. the next afternoon. I drove down to the rail yards late the next evening, circling in my truck, looking and waiting for Canada. After a few hours, Canada had still not shown up. Disappointed and worried, I returned home. Late that night the phone rang. It was Canada. He told me a horror story about how he had hopped the wrong train and got caught on a "bone rattler" all the way to Green River, Wyoming. A bone rattler is a freight car whose suspension has given out. It rumbles, sways, and vibrates like crazy and pulverizes anything inside. Canada was pounded in the rail car until he passed out, only to wake up a state away. I got out of bed and headed south. I had to drive through the night and back to get my replacement to work on time.

We rolled in a couple of hours late. We had plenty of time to polish the story, and we just blamed our tardiness on a missed connection at the Salt Lake City airport. I introduced Canada to the administration and staff and they all seemed to take the bait. Canada had decided to wear a Crocodile Dundee hat he had found in a Dumpster, and it seemed to be just the trick to make it all believable. We went down into the park and I gave him a crash course in animal husbandry. I wanted my friend to be safe, but not so apparently apprehensive that it would be unbelievable. I came up with ways he could get by, but there is an element of risk anytime you work around wild animals.

I loaded my suitcase with flip-flops, tank tops, and sunscreen, and headed off to the Caribbean. As I pulled away, I felt a bit worried, but somehow I knew that I could count on Canada no matter what.

When I returned after my fun in the sun, I could not believe my eyes. Canada had taken the charade to another level. Not only did he exceed my expectations, he impressed the park's owner, too. Canada had been offered a full-time job!

But there was a problem. Canada was not a U.S. citizen, nor did he hold any valid identification to fill out the forms for employment. Up until then, the entire staff knew him only as Canada and asked no questions. When it came down to it, Canada came up with an I.D. out of nowhere. I didn't know where it came from, but the photo looked nothing like him. It was worth a try, though. The name on the I.D. was Charles something. When we sat down at the desk with the owner and filled out the paperwork, I giggled when I said to Canada, "Hey, Chucky, it is sure nice to have you around full time." He glared at me without the slightest bit of humor on his face. Canada spent the next year working at the park. Along the way, I taught him as much as I could about the animals, and he really seemed to enjoy it. But after a while, there was a wildness in Canada that could not be contained in a nine-to-five job. One morning Canada disappeared, and his days as a wildlife expert were finished. His loyalty will never be forgotten, and the legend of Canada or Charles what's his name will live on among the ranks of the wildlife community forever.

I WAS ONCE CALLED THE GRIZZLY COWBOY BY SOMEONE WHO saw me ride on Brutus's back like a horse. With my upbringing, it's sort of fitting. I have had horses and bears, and I love a good Montana-grown angus steak, but I don't blame the wolves for liking them, too. I'm not a big fan of clear-cut logging, but I live in a house made out of wood. I have chosen to speak for those who have spoken to me ever since I can remember. Even though they lack verbal expression, they still have plenty to say.

CHAPTER 3
THE MAGNET
My Animal Connection

E VER SINCE I CAN REMEMBER, ANIMALS HAVE DEMANDED
my attention. It started with grasshoppers. I was three years
old, stumbling around through the fields that surrounded
my hometown of East Helena. As I walked hand in hand
with my grandma Lillian, I would periodically let go and
desperately try and catch them, they were so colorful and
unique. My curiosity fueled my desire to capture them even
further, so I watched them carefully, trying to figure out
their patterns. I would watch which way they jumped and
what made them jump.

Trial and error, over and over again I would make my
attempt, each time getting closer, learning, beginning to

understand their moves, their strengths, and their weaknesses. Just then, one would hop from the depths of the timothy, brome, and spotted knapweed and perch on my arm. I would look at every detail of its shiny body, watching it twitch and move. I admired its metallic highlights and its strong outer armor that resembled a knight. I didn't catch the grasshopper, it captured me.

After the grasshoppers, it was a muskrat named Marvin my family had on its property. There was an irrigation ditch that cut through the yard of my childhood home. Prickly Pear Creek fed the waterway that ran for miles out to flood some farmer's alfalfa field. I would walk down the broken concrete sidewalk to a footbridge that crossed the water. There I would sit anxiously in the shade of the cottonwood trees and wait for Marvin to appear.

I learned that if I sat long enough, his little brown head would pop up from under the water. Every time I caught a glimpse, a small shot of adrenaline shot through me. This was the beginning of an addiction. I would see him swimming with a mouth full of grass, back and forth to his den in the bank. If I made the slightest move, he would disappear with a splash back under the slow-moving murky water and he would likely not return. As patient as I could be at the age of five, I would try harder and harder to remain motionless, realizing that it would pay off. The longer I could hold still, the more of a show Marvin would give me. I enjoyed the seconds of viewing I would have, and I would relay the moment to my parents in excitement.

Over the next couple of years, my obsession with Marvin continued to grow. My family saw my passion for animals and were supportive. Sometimes I would grow impatient for Marvin the muskrat and start picking peppermint from the edge of the stream. Marvin would suddenly step up on the bank of the irrigation ditch next to me. It would often startle me because he would be really close, which was quite a departure from our previous little "game." We would stare at each other as he preened his perfect mottled brown fur, rubbing his little paws over his face then down his sides, repeating it over and over. I was hypnotized by his actions, and I took in every detail. Then as quickly as he came, he would slip down the grassy slope, and with a plop would swim on down the ditch. I always wondered if he was just as curious about the funny-looking kid who spent hours trying to see him, soon realized I was harmless, and then decided to come over and see what the heck I was all about.

Later in life I witnessed animals reacting to humans without fear in both Alaska and Africa. This is a result of protection, or the fact that the animal has never seen a human before. In either case, they look at us as one of "them," not as an outside predator or a destroyer, although if they are predators themselves, they often look at us as easy prey.

Several years ago, while on foot with a group in Botswana, we walked across vast open lands among various types of antelope and zebra. They rarely lifted their heads from grazing to give us a second glance. We were just a troop of baboons, or something similar in their minds. But just like them, we had our eyes open for predators. It was weighing quite heavily on my mind as I scanned the surrounding thicket for signs of danger. Just a few weeks before our walk, the camp that we were staying at had been devastated by tragedy. The cook was out picking jackal berries to make a pie for the camp's staff. As he bent over in the thick brush picking the berries that had fallen from a tree, a large male lion attacked and killed him. The rest of the staff heard his cries but could not get there in time. They shot the lion for his actions. Though the lion looked at the cook as if he were just another meal and all involved were playing their own parts on the landscape, this event rocked me and made me question myself and my own relationship with animals. The lion was named Brutus.

The universe moves in a perfectly synchronized pattern. Everything dances gracefully within it, and we humans stand on the edge of the dance floor in amazement, often too shy to cut in. Some try to cut in too early; they don't take time to watch and learn the intricate steps and timing. Those who are impatient and step onto the floor prematurely are often mowed down and dragged back to the sidelines. There, people either try to learn more about the rhythm, or they immerse themselves deeply into society, hiding from the wild behind walls and man-made laws.

I don't believe I was born with an edge or advantage in this dance per se. In fact, we are all born with the ability to dance the dance, for we are a part of it. Maybe I just recognized it early on, for I was immersed in it from the minute I learned to crawl, while others are taught to ignore it, and are quickly swept into the patterns of life that turn their back on our innate animal instinct. Though I have had my share of stumbles and falls, I tapped into my groove early on. I learned to listen, and my primal language was calibrated, attuning me to a way of walking the earth in peace and in cadence with all that exists.

When you don't have to worry about stepping on nature's toes, you can look around, listen, and learn without fear or an agenda. There is so much to discover when you don't have to watch your feet and listen to the music at the same time. You understand that you are part of it all and it's where you belong. The song never changes, and it's remained the same forever. The dance of society changes frequently, and those who cower in its beat have to adjust constantly, never truly catching up. It's an awkward place to be, and those who have found comfort in its binds are like a bird in a cage who is too afraid to fly away when you open its door, and these people often want to destroy all that is wild, savage, and pure. I think it is this mind-set of limitless grace that has aided me in my lifelong quest to interact with and understand animals, and in turn, connect back to society and act as a link for better education and understanding.

By now it is clear that I have been drawn toward animals since I can remember, but even more fascinating, I have found that animals have in turn been drawn toward me. As creatures, we humans have been so detached from our animal roots after generations of civilized living that we have buried deep within us some valuable instinctual tools. Have you ever noticed that when a stranger walks into your home, the dog runs up to him and the kids seem to love him? There is a reason. It may be subtle, but it exists. Both the dog and the kids are still keenly attuned to body language. Animals, not able to speak, depend on it. Children, not yet affected by the prejudice and "norms" of society, are still close to their primordial roots. This stranger's intentions ride with him like a billboard whether he knows it or not. It just takes that trained eye, or in the kid's case, that core instinctual sense, to read it.

It's hard to be explicit about the exact body language but perhaps it can best be illustrated in a story. A pack of wolves was moving in on a large elk herd one winter morning in the Lamar Valley of Yellowstone National Park. In most cases, wolves seek out the sick, old, or weak for a kill, but today they singled out a large, healthy-looking bull. This was going against all of the norms of a wolf hunt. Or was it? After a short chase and struggle, the large bull was killed, and mostly devoured by the pack. Baffled by the wolves' strange behavior, some biologists took tissue and bone marrow samples from the bull elk's carcass. When the test results came back, they revealed that this bull had a strange blood disease and had in fact been very sick. The obvious signs didn't show to the "unaware" eye of the onlooking biologists as the wolves picked out their dinner, but the wolves knew it from the beginning purely on subtle instinctual clues. Their "eye" depends on this for survival, and this "sixth sense" has been so finely calibrated that they could pick out even the slightest signs of weakness in a otherwise deceptively healthy-looking specimen.

Despite my professed ability to walk the earth in harmony with nature, when it comes to Mother Nature's aquatic environment, I sink like a rock. When you grow up in Montana, the lakes and rivers are frozen most of the year, and in the four months they are not, the water is simply frigid. Swimming wasn't a big childhood pastime for me, but come summer time, we did go canoeing.

My brother Jeremy, my dad, and I planned a canoe trip up

the Missouri River one year, when I was about eight. Our destination was a historic Lewis and Clark encampment, a riverside location near York, Montana, where the explorers spent the night during their expedition. I had already learned about a good portion of their adventures and I was excited about the prospect of the journey and reliving a bit of history, but my fear of the water left me a little nervous.

We pulled out just as the sun rose on the Little Belt Mountains. Clinging to the side of the boat like a cat dangling over a pack of dogs, I feared the deep, dark waters below and was very happy I had my life jacket on. Every time my brother wiggled around, rocking the canoe, my claws would sink deeper into its side.

It was a warm August morning with not a cloud in the sky. As we paddled up the river, I tried to imagine how the explorers must have felt as they laid eyes on that exact landscape nearly two hundred years earlier.

As images swirled in my mind I thought I saw a Shoshone warrior in the limestone cliffs above, watching as the three white men drifted into unexplored territory. Then, my water-loving brother rocked the boat again, snapping me out of my dream, and the lone warrior turned back into a perched turkey vulture, still watching us attentively.

The rhythmic dipping of the paddles gently rocked me back into the nineteenth century once my anxiety abated. Then, suddenly, a sea monster seemed to lurch from the seaweed, splashing violently. My heart again pounded, but as I hung on for dear life, I realized that it was only a large school of carp feeding near the surface that our approaching vessel scared away.

I was glad to see the inlet ahead as we circled the bend in the slow-moving river. As the canoe slid ashore, we quickly unloaded our gear and prepared to set up camp. My dad asked me to gather firewood, so I grabbed my Daisy Red Rider lever-action BB gun and headed off into the wilds, wishing only that I had a coonskin cap on my head. Like a brave pioneer, musket in hand, I crept through the nearby pines. I had some hunting to do before I was going to gather anything, obviously. The scrub juniper and sagebrush left a potpourri of aromas on the fresh summer breeze. I listened carefully for any quarry as I crept down the game trail. I watched for native scouts, and would stop and give hand signals to my imaginary expedition party that followed closely behind.

Suddenly, ahead of me, lurking on the limb of a tree, I saw a beast that would feed me and my entire expedition crew for the rest of the week. A chipmunk. I crept forward down the trail, continuing to give my hunting party hand signals.

The chipmunk was unaware as I raised my musket and took aim. My Daisy Red Ryder gave a pop and the little chipmunk scurried away, wounded. I didn't want the little guy to suffer and I mostly just wanted to bring the chipmunk back to my dad so he would be proud of me, and maybe I'd show up my brother in the process.

So I tracked the beast deeper into the woods. I saw him slip away into the brush, took one last fleeting shot, and missed. Though I realized the chipmunk was likely not wounded at all and was taking me on a wild-goose chase, I still got down on my hands and knees, gun in hand, and crawled through the brush after him. I caught a glimpse of him once again and increased the speed of my pursuit. As he neared the base of a large juniper bush where I had last seen him, I was startled to find myself face-to-face with a giant prairie rattlesnake! Only a foot from his face, I looked into his eyes as he flicked his tongue while his tail buzzed like a chainsaw.

Frozen in fear and hypnotized by the moment, I stayed completely still. I knew I was in a dangerous situation, one I had never been in before, and it was time to act on my instincts. As slowly as possible, I backed away barely more than a millimeter at a time, never losing direct eye contact with the serpent, never even blinking an eye.

We watched each other, breathing slowly, each waiting for the other to make a move. After what seemed like an hour, I finally reached a distance where I felt safe. The snake was still coiled to strike. I raised my rifle and put the sights between his eyes. Oh, how my dad was going to be proud, I thought. I pulled the trigger and the snake violently flipped around from the direct hit. I reloaded and fired again and again until the snake was motionless. I remember crawling to the snake and picking it up delicately, worried that its venom would leak out onto my arm but still very curious because I had never touched or been this close to a rattlesnake before. I scooped him up and headed back to camp, pleased with my upgrade over the scrawny chipmunk. I remember my dad's eyes as I rounded the corner with a four-and-a-half-foot-long rattlesnake in my arms and said "Hey, Dad, look what I got for dinner." Most parents would have been surprised, but my dad knew me well.

So, with a smile, he happily skinned and gutted the snake,

and my brother, my dad, and I enjoyed "rattlesnake kebabs" around the campfire that night. I sat there, as proud as Lewis and Clark must have felt long ago, eating the quarry of my kill, feeding my family, like a true expedition leader!

A few years later, on yet another trek with my dad, we found ourselves standing on the top of a mountain ridge. We had been hiking for most of the morning. It was a perfect summer day, the kind of weather that allowed us to push higher in elevation than we ever had before. I caught my breath and stared out over the valley at its vast beauty. I caught a movement out of the corner of my eye. It was a large male mountain goat. He, too, had just reached the ridge top and was also taking in the view. It was one of my first times seeing a mountain goat, and at nine years old I wasn't much bigger than this giant billy.

The goat turned on the ridge line and began to walk toward me. I stood there motionless with my dad behind me. The goat continued until he had walked right up to me. There we stood, nose to nose, looking into each other's eyes. His long, black daggerlike horns contrasted with his snowy white fur. His eyes were noble and kind. I could see his nostrils flex as he sniffed me and investigated. The goat's proximity to me alarmed my father, who waved his arms and shooed the goat away. The goat scooted off, but only because of my dad's actions. I was sad to see the goat go, as I was just beginning to get a good look at him. We discussed why we thought the mountain goat came up to me. "There must have been something wrong with him," seemed to be the verdict, but deep down, even as a child I had my doubts. I truly believed he was as curious about me as I was about him. This would not be the first time or the last time that this sort of wild animal interaction would happen to me.

Fast-forward twenty years. I often drive by an agricultural area and will look out in a field and see cows, horses, and deer all eating together. It gets me thinking about the decisions that the deer had to make to let their guard down and approach these two very different species. The deer must watch the horses and cattle from afar at first and analyze their demeanor to learn a bit about these creatures monopolizing all this tasty grass. They must make a decision that concludes that the grazing creatures are harmless. Does the deer know these animals' history? Does the deer know any more beyond their own observations of the other animals? Not likely, but the projection of intentions, coupled with past history of similar species interaction over time, allows the deer to approach. And this very same analysis allows the cattle and horses to identify the deer as an animal of no risk.

Do animals see this in certain individual people? Do individual people project a "harmless" aura or vibe? We have front-facing eyes, canine-type teeth, and move like a predator, while prey animals have eyes literally on the sides of their heads so they can see almost 360 degrees to watch for approaching predators. Yet some of us are accepted by animals in a way that others are not. Animals frequently accept me, but I have seen the opposite many times. Someone will walk into the wildlife park, and all the dogs bark, and an ominous air falls over everyone. This person must reek of something that creates anxiety. Without speaking a word, his or her intentions and mind-set are obvious to all.

It was late October, and my father and I were tracking a large bull elk through shin-deep snow. I was a spry young teenager and climbed the mountain just like the elk we followed. We could hear the same bull elk two gullies over, bugling and grunting, as we continued to close the gap. We were walking up a very steep hillside that had burned down a couple of years earlier in a human-caused forest fire. New little aspen saplings covered the slope and made it difficult to maneuver through the snow.

I led the tracking and zigged and zagged looking for the fresh bull tracks among the hundreds of day-old elk tracks. I was young, but I knew my tracks by now. I stopped to sort out a confusing junction of tracks and to scan the surrounding slopes with my binoculars for any additional evidence of the big bull elk, when I felt something slide up onto my boot. I glanced down in astonishment. Coiled on my boot was a four-foot-long rattlesnake. At least this time it wasn't inches from my face, and I knew just what to do. I was standing in snow, high on a mountain hillside, in an area that should almost *never* have rattlesnakes, and yet one had found me and was using me for warmth on this chilly day. I held still. I was in a precarious situation and I had to calculate my next move very carefully.

I looked down at the snake and could see that it was cold and moving slower than usual. The poor thing just needed warmth. It had not made it to its den in time and was caught out in an early winter snowstorm. I reached down and grabbed the snake securely behind the head and walked it up to a rocky cliff outcropping. There I let the snake go and watched it slither into a crack in the boulders. My dad scratched his head as he watched his teenage son have another bizarre animal encounter. After all, the snake had not cozied up to him, who was bigger and therefore warmer. I sat there and tried to digest what had just happened, but even though I couldn't make sense of it, my body felt alive with some sort of intoxicating charge. I still had a big bull elk to track and realized that this magnetism works both ways.

These stories are just a handful among many from my childhood. The experiences and interactions I had with animals as a child sowed the seed that grew into the desire to spend the rest of my life working with animals. It was these moments that pushed me to volunteer at wildlife sanctuaries, to study wildlife biology, and to pursue a career that involved working close to animals. I never wanted to be a fireman, a policeman, or a doctor. My life path was clear to me from the beginning.

Over my lifetime these moments have blessed my life. I have learned to recognize them as special moments and I try to gather as much as I can from each of them when they occur. I have studied animals all of my life, and this experience has led me to my relationship with Brutus today. The knowledge I've gleaned has allowed me to cultivate my natural abilities and has given me the gift of a peculiar window into the soul of a grizzly bear.

CHAPTER 4
DESPERATE CRIES

D ESPERATE CRIES DO NOT GO UNANSWERED, AS WHEN baby Brutus was trapped beneath his mother.

I was in my late twenties when I decided to go for a long hike in search of grizzly bears. High in a hanging valley just outside the northern border of Yellowstone National Park, I found a cow elk starving from the winter famine. She was emaciated and weak. Her body trembled as she struggled to get to her feet. I struggled with my compassion. As I watched her suffer, I asked myself, "Do I just let nature take its course or do I give her mercy from her pain"? At what point did I, as a human filled with empathy, but still an animal, become exempt from the laws of nature? This is a question, or a choice, that we all must examine, whether out in the wild, like me, or caring for a terminally ill loved one who has asked to be let go, despite our own wishes to keep trying, at all costs, to deny the inevitable.

That day, the early spring sunshine warmed my body. I breathed the fresh cool mountain air. It seemed so unfair. As I watched the elk try to hold off the clutches of death, my heart ached for her. She would stand, stumble, and then violently crash to the ground. This happened over and over again for an hour, until finally she fell over a large Douglas fir log, so exhausted she could no longer get up. There she lay, so weak, trapped under the weight of her own body. She lay there in silence. The elk and I could hear only the wind touching the trees and the babble of the creek below. Her herd had moved on from her now in search of food, and despite her determined spirit, I could see loneliness overtake her.

She made one final burst to get up but then fell quickly and hard against the log. She bellowed out in fear, a cry only a creature in absolute desperation will make. Her cry echoed against the amphitheater of distant snow-covered peaks. I knew her herd had probably heard her all those miles away, but they could do nothing for her. She took several deep, slow breaths, her ribs and hip bones jutting out through her skin. Just when I thought she had made peace with death, loneliness would make its assault once more, and in a panicked state, she would cry out.

I felt awful as I tried to put myself in her situation and think how she must have felt, alone at the proverbial end of the world—not only the obvious pain of starving, but the torture of helplessness and loneliness. In one quick move, I rushed down the slope to her side. She looked up at me. Her eyes were a beautiful, dark brown almond shape. She had long eyelashes, and I could see the absolute kindness in her soul. My inner beast then took over. I glanced around and located a boulder just light enough to lift. I raised it high over my head. I looked her in the eye and said, "Sorry, girl," and then crushed her skull, ending the misery.

Her misery, or mine?

In my selfish, egocentric, human mind, I had a brief moment of satisfaction in having done something good. I then realized that I had made a huge mistake.

It had been a severely harsh winter that year. The Yellowstone region had received more snowfall that season than it had in over ten years. This kind of winter usually makes a powerful dent on the grass-eating ungulates, while giving the predators and scavengers a winter of ease. Most would believe that the elk, bison, and deer would starve and die during the harshest part of the winter, during mid-January, when the temperatures are well below zero and the snow is the deepest. But most of the actual death occurs just as the grips of winter are letting up and it would seem hope was on its way. Often most of the snow has melted, the temperatures are warming, and spring is closing in. The wary, hard-wintered creatures get their first bites of green grass, and it would seem that they had made it through. It is at this time, when they eat the rich shoots of grass, that their bodies simply give up after months of deprivation. The vitamin-filled grasses are too rich for their system and often give them diarrhea, and this additional stress and dehydration is just enough to kill them. It is interesting how mother nature has timed herself.

As the ungulates are dying, usually in early April, the coyote and wolf pups are born, and grizzly bear cubs are emerging from their warm dens. The carcasses of the dying or dead elk and bison are often a welcome first meal to these new additions to the mountains, or else give vital nutrients to the mothers who now have many mouths to feed and need additional nutritional reserves.

It is a highly sought-after prize. One elk carcass, even an emaciated one, can feed a grizzly family for almost a week. The bears often use their keen noses to locate the now stinky carcasses. But usually when the decaying body is old enough to smell, it has already been visited by other scavengers who have happened upon them. The others have often eaten most of the carcass, or else present an unneeded confrontation to the arriving grizzly.

A bear will often come upon a carcass and do what amounts to a cost-benefit analysis. They are true opportunists. If the fight will likely expend less energy than the meal will yield, then they are more than happy to tangle with any creature. This is risky and can have consequences. Fights often lead to wasted crucial energy, injuries, even death. But there is an easier way. If that grizzly has the chance to hear a starving animal crying out just before it dies, it will often go to it and then kill it itself and will then have the entire carcass to itself.

Few animals, with the exception of a brave wolverine or an entire wolf pack, will try to run off a grizzly, and a hungry one at that. When it came to my supposed mercy killing of the starving elk, I soon realized I was doing nobody any favors. My selfish human attitude could have prevented a much-needed meal to several creatures who would have heard the cries. This became even more evident when I returned to that site three weeks later. I went in hope of seeing a fat, happy grizzly bear. Instead I found a rotten, untouched elk carcass. Whether it was left alone because of my earlier presence or the senses of other animals, it was well beyond edible for any animal, wasted and tainted by my own self-proclaimed justice.

Here's another story. My father and I were on our way home after a long day of elk hunting for that year's family meat supply. Though we killed nothing that day, we were happy to be in the warmth of the old Nissan pickup truck, listening to the same golden oldies cassette tape for at least the hundredth time. I was fourteen years old.

We were mostly just happy to be together. I was wearing my typical hunting garb. Over my long underwear, I wore a hooded pullover bearing the name of my high school, Helena High School. Over that I wore an insulated flannel shirt. I wore an old pair of jeans and a pair of football cleats, for added traction on the steep mountainsides. Though they were not your typical mountaineering boot, I had made each of them waterproof by adding a plastic Wonder Bread bag under each wool sock. My hunting outfit was probably all purchased from the Salvation Army, a mismatch of impractical clothing, but it seemed to do the trick. Bouncing in our seats down the mountain path, we both daydreamed of the delicious dinner of steak and potatoes and the hot fireplace we'd sit next to once we got back home. Little did I know that I wasn't going to be seeing any of it that night.

As the sun dipped behind the mountains, snow began to fall in the new twilight. As we rounded the corner of a small two-track road, there in the middle of the road stood a bull elk. My dad brought the truck to a quick stop. My competitive mind superseded any logic. I jumped from the truck, leaving the passenger door wide open, and pursued the elk, who had now trotted into the trees, spooked by the squeak of the brakes.

Leaving the safety of the truck, and the faint melody of some Motown hit behind me, I could see the elk up ahead. As I drew nearer, he slipped out of sight into the shadows of the lodgepole pines. I walked to where I had last seen him, saw him again for a fleeting moment, and then he disappeared into the dark forest again.

This pattern happened three or four more times. I was so concentrated on my carnivorous pursuit that I never took the opportunity to contemplate where he was leading me. As I crested an open ridge, I stared in disbelief. In the dim light, I could just make out a small mountain basin, covered in short moose-browsed willows, beaver ponds, and marsh grass. An old rickety barbed wire fence hung on one last remaining rotten post, like a rusty evil vine, adding to the haunting scene. The open land was hugged by the ever-darkening forest that surrounded it. I now realized I was nowhere I had ever been before. It was almost completely dark, and I was lost.

Panic rushed through my body like a wildfire. I spotted a high nob and thought I could sprint to the top of it, to try and get a last-second view in the fading light and find my bearings. As I reached the top, the scene shattered any chance

I thought I might have had. I recognized nothing. The snow began to fall harder, and dusk settled in like a depressing fog.

I screamed at the top of my lungs and chastised myself for being stupid. Nonetheless, I screamed over and over again. "Help me" echoed through the valleys below. Loneliness attacked me. I felt desperate and panicked even more. I took off, running blindly through the dark forest. I tripped over dead fallen trees, often slamming to the hard, frozen forest floor, knocking the wind out of myself. I would then get up and yell. I started to cry, and in a desperate frenzy, I would repeat the process over and over again.

This went on for almost an hour. I would only pause for a few brief seconds to listen. There was nothing, only the pounding of my heart, my frantic breathing, and the moaning winds of the approaching blizzard. Finally, fatigue and exhaustion took over my body. I was soaked in sweat, dangerously wet now that the temperature was plummeting. I could not scream now, I could only let out a feeble whimper. I was alone, ashamed of myself, and terrified.

I slowly dragged myself to the base of a giant ponderosa pine. Its limbs stretched out from its trunk like the ceiling of a cathedral. Somehow this ancient tree brought me a small bit of peace. As I lay in the blanket of decades of fallen pine needles, I thought of all the nights and blizzards this wise old tree had seen. I propped my back up against its massive trunk, pulled a layer of pine needles over my energy-drained legs for added insulation, and helplessly wept like a baby. I was drenched and cold. When I wiggled my toes to keep them warm, the bread sacks would crinkle, sounding like a campfire I pretended was there, and somehow I felt the warmth of the flames. The snow began to blanket the ground, producing an ominous glow in the unpredictable surroundings. Like a sentry, I stood guard over my life, vigilantly listening for any approaching danger.

I knew that desperate cries in the wilderness do not go unanswered; I just hoped mine would be answered by the right being. I was stirred by a distant, unidentifiable sound. I must have dozed off. I wasn't sure how much time had gone by but it seemed that most of the night had passed. I listened attentively but could hear only the unforgiving storm. Was my mind playing tricks on me? Was it the call of the cold ghost of false hope? Again, I heard the noise, a faint, undefinable echo in the unknown landscape.

This time I was sure it was real. A last bit of energy rushed into my limp body. I stood up and stumbled in the direction of the sound. As I made my way through the maze of the unknown woods, I could tell I was getting closer. My legs felt like they weighed two hundred pounds apiece. I dragged them like anchors over every tree snag along the way.

A good amount of time passed without my hearing any more sounds. I started to feel stupid again, fooled by my delirious mind. I cussed at myself and missed my wise old tree and the imaginary campfire beside it.

Suddenly, like a crack of lightning from heaven, I heard my father's stern voice. "Casey, what the hell are you doing?" I fell into his arms and cried uncontrollably in absolute thankfulness. Tears of relief streamed down our faces as we walked back, following his tracks in the snow toward the waiting truck. He had spent the whole night looking for me.

We never spoke about it again. He was happy I was safe, and he knew I had been punished by my experience and had learned a very hard lesson. I was lucky, and I hold that moment dear, like a trophy on my shelf of life experiences. That night my torturous cries were answered by my own kind, but they surely also fell on the ears of others who wouldn't have rescued me. What if a different animal had answered my cries that night and crushed my skull, putting me out of my misery?

CHAPTER **5**

THE TRACKER

THE WINDOWS OF A CLASSROOM HAVE ALWAYS TORMENTED me. As I sat in my uncomfortably rigid wood-and-metal desk, I stared out the window at the Elkhorn Mountain range. I would fidget as I looked, wishing and wondering, climbing ridges with my eyes, and conjuring up places that I wanted to explore.

On a lucky day, I would be snapped out of my ruminations by the sound of my name being called. My teacher would stand with a slip of paper in her hand and tell me that my father was in the school office waiting for me. I was excused for the rest of the day!

Now, when most kids got this news, they were going to

the dentist or to the doctor, or else something awful had arisen. Not me. I would throw my books into my desk and race out of the classroom with excitement. It was fall, and it was hunting season. Though I usually only got to go on weekends, my dad would often go on weekdays. And if he came to get me—and I am sure my teacher would not have approved—it was tracking time! I have a skill my dad recognized at a very young age: the art of the tracker, the uncanny way of being able to follow or move through the forest as an animal would, understanding to the level of nearly becoming. I learned at a very young age out of curiosity that if I simply looked and listened, the clues were there. Even the mightiest of beasts may leave only the slightest trace, but they do leave something.

And so my dad would come and get me out of school to track wounded animals for him. I learned a lot from animals over the years while following the blood trails they left in their confusion and anguish. In their desperation to running frantically from the approaching darkness of death, I learned from their mistakes. I learned their patterns in the flight of fear, like an atlas, traced on the forest floor in crimson red.

Not only did I track wounded animals, I followed any tracks I found, at any given time, anytime I was outdoors. I knew that the tracks would lead to the animal who made them. Following old tracks meant long days without results, and in that, I may have found patience, but more than that, I learned the importance of how to identify a fresh track so as not to waste my time. A track will deteriorate at a very specific rate in certain conditions. There are many variables, such as the sun, wind, or what the track was left in (dirt, mud, snow, etc.). But in time, after looking at thousands of tracks and cross-referencing them with results, it became a simple science. I would make my own track next to the one that I was examining. I would blow on my own track to mimic the exposure to the natural wind of the track in question. I would use every trick I had up my sleeve to determine the age of the track. It was essential to know when the animal passed through, what time of day, and a number of other factors if I wanted to get an understanding of its current location. Following tracks can be simple in the mud or snow. The animals leave evidence of every step imprinted in their wake. But under other conditions, there are places where the tracks just end, where nothing visible is left behind. This is when you must improvise on patterns of behavior that you have learned from past experiences.

One lucky day, when my father had excused me from school, I was following tracks of an elk who'd been wounded by an arrow my dad had launched with his bow. I was like a hound on a hot trail when suddenly the track disappeared altogether. I had zig-zagged trying to recross the track, picking up the blood trail again, but in the end I lifted my eyes from the ground and just thought and walked like an elk. Three miles further on, I stood in the elk's tracks again. My dad was amazed, but it had been as simple as following the tracks of my instincts and the collective trail of all my experiences.

Although Brutus is quite different from an elk, he is still a creature open to the world of emotion and instinct, and having an open mind that took a lifetime to develop is the reason I can have a relationship with him. Listening. Truly listening to him. Following him. Letting him run wild, and understanding his patterns, his nature, his needs, desires, and preferences.

Animals are as expert at tracking as we humans are. They, too, analyze and store patterns of behavior. I know Brutus tracks me as I have tracked him. He knows my habits, he knows what I am thinking, often reacting to me before I even ask. It's classic conditioning, and with the amount of time and situations we have been in together, we have honed it to a precise understanding of one another.

I have been following grizzly bears around for over fifteen years in the wild and for the past eight years at the Montana Grizzly Encounter. This opportunity to apply my experiences from one to the other has helped me develop a deeply complex cross-reference of understanding.

One such example is the fascinating relationship between the raven and the grizzly bear.

Over and over again this relationship has helped me find an elusive bear from miles away. While on a filming expedition to Botswana's Okavango Delta, I met a seasoned tracker named Julius. He had tracked nearly every species of animal in Africa and was a true artist of the craft. Julius taught me an old adage that I will keep with me forever: "If you want to know where the big animals are, watch the little animals." Once I started to apply this, the results were astonishing. I once lost the tracks of a grizzly bear on a ridge top, and glanced in every direction, wondering which way the bear had gone.

As I stood there, a raven surfed the wind, its wings rigid, as it glided in large circles over the vast wilderness below.

Suddenly it changed direction, veering away from its glide, and dipped down to give something a second look. Now I knew where the grizzly was. In fact, I knew its exact current location, thanks to my black feathered friend. Centuries of these two species interacting has led to an amazing relationship.

Both the raven and the grizzly are scavengers, each with a highly developed sensory system. The raven has an acute sense of sight and the ability to get high above the rugged land to scan for food, and the grizzly has an excellent sense of smell and the mobility and power to unearth anything that might be hidden. I have watched ravens identify and go to grizzly bears as much as I have watched grizzly bears identify and go to ravens. When Brutus is walking anywhere, at the sanctuary or even one time down the street in downtown Denver, I have watched ravens notice him, recognize him as a bear, and come over for a closer look. They assume that where there is a bear, there is food, and that is usually the case, but there is no preference between wild bears and captive.

I will watch ravens fly over the sanctuary, sometimes hundreds of feet above. The birds are often flying over in a straight line, as if they are going on a mission somewhere. But when the bears come into view, they can't help but swoop down and give their big fuzzy friends a second look. When I first went to the moth feeding sites, a very specific area far above the tree line where army cutworm moths congregate, along with the bears that eat them, I found it often difficult to spot grizzly bears among the boulders if they were not moving. But after a period of observation, I began to notice that each bear came with its own raven entourage. The gang of pesky black birds would hover around the bear just waiting for any leftovers or stray moths to pop out. And the bear didn't mind. In fact, anytime the ravens reacted in fear, the bear would lift its head and look around. The bear's raven posse was acting as a lookout while the bear had its head buried in the rocks sniffing for moths. They were truly helping each other out, a textbook case of a symbiotic relationship.

Another time that I personally integrated this unique bond in my grizzly viewing actually caught me by surprise. I was standing in a thick stand of Douglas firs looking over a large sagebrush plateau. About a quarter mile away I could see an unusually large grizzly walking across the opening, moving slightly away from me but not necessarily feeling threatened. I wanted to get a better look, but there was no way I would ever catch up to him. An idea popped into my mind, and all at once, I let out my best "raven call." The bear heard me and stopped. I thought that my poor attempt at mimicry would certainly lead to his sprinting away, but I tried it a second time just in case. As soon as I let out my second "caw caw" he came straight at me! In this bear's mind there was likely something dead on the edge of the forest, and the bear was going to chase away some birds and maybe a coyote and have a nice meal. As he moved within thirty yards of me, I felt the wind at my back, and as fast as he had come, he spun around on a dime and disappeared into the forest. The stinky scent of human was lifted off my body and carried on the breeze, trumping my poorly mimicked raven sounds.

In a grizzly bear's world, the sense of smell comes first,

THE STORY OF BRUTUS

then the sense of hearing, and finally the sense of sight. Grizzly bear rule number one: when you are wandering through bear country, always be aware of the direction of the wind.

Brutus has not made much of a living eating rotten carcasses. He has not learned to associate a raven with a food source. He rarely gives the noisy birds a second look. I speculate that little bear cubs in the wild learn this skill from their mother. After countless times of having a full belly in the presence of their raven friends, basic conditioning must kick in. In an interesting turnabout, ravens have learned that if they land next to Brutus, they can surely count on a sumptous meal. Instead of a putrid dead animal, they might find a baked sockeye salmon filet with a lemon garnish. Brutus has good taste.

CHAPTER **6**

LOST LANGUAGE

THE "LANGUAGE" BRUTUS AND I HAVE DEVELOPED OVER the years is a primal one. Imagine two people who want to communicate but who do not know each other's language. They struggle, speaking slowly to one another, but it is no use. In their frustration, they succumb to their deepest language, and start giving hand signals, making sounds, and acting like cave men. They begin to understand each other. They are speaking the same language. As animals, we possess an even deeper language, our animal language, the same language all animals on this earth inherently possess.

When confronted with the same challenges as the two people described above, but it is you and an animal who are in linguistic gridlock, you desperately dig deeper into yourself for tools that will get results. Gradually they will surface, and you can develop a language that you were born with as an animal. It takes great desire to reach back to that level, and it takes great practice to develop an understanding of that language. With patience and passion, you soon find yourself exercising something deep from within your soul, and discovering how to tap into this ancient behavior brings you closer to being truly present. You are now at the root of your being, and it is as pure and as organic as anything in your life. It can be extremely energizing. Existing in this place is what it is to be truly alive in the moment. You don't have time to think about the past or the future. Your mind doesn't whirl in chaotic thought. You are living in that moment only, just as the animals do. It's a place where you can listen for silence, and find it. It's the ultimate form of meditation, and it comes with no lies and no excuses. It's that cherished moment when time seems to disappear and wasted thought is erased. We feel moments like this once in a while in our regular life. We tap into it during sex, or it bares its head during an emergency. It is primal. When you immerse yourself in the pure and present "wild," speaking the language comes with its share of mortal responsibility. A misspoken word in the company of those who speak it every day can be a fatal mistake.

Brutus and I have experienced linguistic gridlock many times. We would look at each other helplessly, then one of us would do something, and the other would respond. It was awkward in the beginning, but over time it became easier. It was trial and error, and we would take turns throwing a fit and stomping around in disappointment. Then there were those magical moments when we understood each other. Those moments cascaded into more such moments and took us to the next level. Exercising our fellowship in this manner rejuvenates my soul and I imagine it does the same for Brutus.

One of the most essential things I worked on with Brutus was teaching him to walk on a leash. It has to be done the right way, because the last thing you want is to be tethered to an upset, nine-hundred-pound grizzly. When I introduced him to the leash, it went against every bit of what he had learned up until that point. As a little cub, Brutus was mostly spoiled and did whatever he wanted. Now I was going to show him that sometimes he had to go where *I* wanted to go. With the help of Ami, one of the Encounter staff, I started him with a harness. Brutus felt confined and did everything he could to get it off. He rolled around, pawing and biting the harness, trying to destroy it. Whenever he relaxed, I would reward him with praise, scratches on his head, and treats. Then he would erupt into another claustrophobic fit and I would stand by patiently waiting for the next respite. After tugging and scratching at the harness for an hour, Brutus finally surrendered. I sat there loving him in his moment of tameness, and sympathized with him about his confining predicament. Brutus is exceptional when it comes to understanding. It didn't take him long to realize that when I invited him to wear a leash it meant we would be going on an adventure. When he sees a leash today, he can hardly contain his excitement.

Every time we are together, there is an opportunity to get

to know each other better. It is an ever-evolving relationship. Figuratively, sometimes I want to go right, and he thinks I mean left, and we walk right into each other. There we stand, face-to-face, realizing we need to try again. We will both take a deep breath and try again, this time with a little hesitation, not in fear, but with respect for one another. When the dots connect, we celebrate that juncture as a new "word" in our language. We have developed a diverse and complex language, one that is hard to explain. Outsiders see the ease of our relationship and often ask if they can work close to Brutus. I am always quick to tell them no. At this point it would be nearly impossible for someone to just step in. It has taken countless hours and days to create the bond Brutus and I share. It would be foolish and irresponsible of me to expose Brutus to strangers. In the likely case that the human was making all the mistakes, Brutus would be punished for it. I must protect my friend.

CHAPTER 7
SCARS

S CARS RIDDLE MY BODY, EACH A TATTOO OF A LESSON learned. I wear them with pride, because each mark of healed flesh provokes a memory, a moment in my life in which I had made a mistake. This tapestry of mended wounds makes me the man I am today. Most of them are hidden away in my heart, soul, and mind. Others stand strong on my skin, a constant reminder of past battles with various beasts.

I have a tear across my right pectoral from the claws of a mountain lion. I have a deep divot in my right calf from the canine of a wolf. I have a gash across my forearm that was left behind from the pressure of a black bear's jaws. I am branded with mistakes I have made—they remind me that I am mortal. Any one of them could have been my last, but for some reason they heal, and I grow, and I always seem to be in search of more. The older I get, the more time passes between visits to the emergency room, evidence of progress and understanding. Walking away from a life-threatening situation is moving, and the days that follow are always a period of reflection.

Brutus and I have never spilled each other's blood, a strong indication of our mutual "education." I have spent more time with Brutus than with all of the other animals I have ever been around combined. The lack of scars produced by Brutus speaks for itself. I would never have accomplished such a peaceful bond with Brutus without a past full of violent lessons.

One such event that deeply affected me happened in the beginning of my career. I was nineteen and working at a wildlife farm that hired out their animals for film and photography. I was young, in awesome shape, and full of energy and excitement. My dream to work with animals was coming true, and I would wake up early every morning excited to get to work. Every day was different and unpredictable. I didn't know if I was going to be on a helicopter flying high into the Bridger Mountains with a snow leopard, or walking a wolverine down to the Shields River for a swim. One thing I did know was that it would never be boring.

The game farm had its own pack of wolves, nine in total. They were wolves that had been purchased as puppies from other game farms or zoos to train for television and film. They all paced anxiously in their individual kennels waiting for their next opportunity to be a pack. When you train a wolf, isolation is often the best way to get them to want to engage with you one on one. Training was mostly work for them, but when they were in a pack it was mostly play. They cherish the social moment. On the days we didn't train them, we would put them into a one-acre enclosure and let them be a pack again. They would chase each other around, faux fight, wrestle, chew on each other, and generally enjoy themselves. The yard was full of growls, snarls, yelps, and whining, all examples of wolf happiness.

It was a typical Montana summer morning. The sky was clear and everything was fresh and crisp. Dew clung to the grass, and the aroma of the forest was amplified. I had just walked each wolf to the exercise pen and left them alone to mingle. I was standing in the equipment shed when I heard a fight break out. Aggressive growls, snarls, and yelping echoed through the surrounding hills as I sprinted through the yard toward the enclosure.

As I approached, the fight had run its course. Tundra, the alpha male, stood off to the side with a light smearing of blood across his face. Dakota, the up-and-coming alpha male, stood in the other corner with the same guilty red markings. Like two prize fighters after an intense round, they breathed heavily and stared at each other across the ring. The rest of the pack paced in chaotic form, confused but excited by the scuffle.

I entered the enclosure to do some preventive maintenance, and to insure that another brawl would not happen, lest a wolf get seriously injured or even killed. The members of the pack were very different from each other. All of them liked me, but some were shyer than others and would take extra attention to catch. I caught Tundra first and returned him to his kennel. He was the leader and likely the instigator of most of the pack action, so I figured that his absence would extinguish most of the conflict. Fights are part of the whole pack dynamic, but it seemed that this one had gotten out of hand.

I returned to the remaining wolves. The pack was still in a highly anxious state. Dakota stood apart from the others, his head held low as if he had just received a beating. He was one of my favorite wolves. Dakota was like a giant puppy when it came to interacting with me. He was a strong, big wolf with piercing yellow eyes. But deep down he was almost like a big lap dog, and he loved to have his belly rubbed.

I squatted down and called to him in a baby voice. He wagged his tail in response and started to squirm over to me in a submissive excitement. When he reached me, something suddenly changed. I remember his eyes first. They were dilated, with only a sliver of the golden yellow color remaining in his now dark, empty, sharklike eyes. We were now face-to-face, and he bared his teeth at me, something he had never done before. I stood up quickly, confused and angry. I yelled at him sternly, "NO!" The sharp word was coupled with the sound of the tearing of heavy denim and flesh from the back of my leg. Denali, another adult male wolf, had just sunk his teeth through my insulated Carhartt overalls into my hamstring. There was more than one shark in this tank. I whirled around and confronted my attacker. Again, I yelled a very unforgiving "NO!" and pointed my finger at him, which was all I could do at this stage.

I was completely baffled by the way the wolves were reacting. Just as I regained my bearings after being bitten, I was suddenly attacked from behind again. This time, when I turned, it was Dakota, the wolf I thought was my biggest ally. I remember the crushing pressure of his massive jaws as they popped through my calf. I was lost in confusion and panic. As I stared into Dakota's empty eyes, I was sucker punched from behind again. When I spun to face what was now a full-on assault, the world went into slow motion. There was no sound, just the ominous image of a pack of eight wolves surrounding me. There was nothing else in the world but me and the ring of savage canines that was closing in.

Their eyes were all dark and emotionless. Their tails flicked back and forth as they each lunged in and took their turn chomping down on my legs. Each time I turned to face a wolf, another attacked me from behind. I screamed for help, but I knew I was alone. All of my co-workers had left for the day. There was no one for miles. My screams became more desperate, my increasing panic only fueling the frenzy of the wolf pack. I kicked and screamed. All I could do was try to keep my balance as each wolf delivered a gripping bite and tried to tug me to the ground. If I were to fall now, I would never get up, certain to die in the maelstrom of a wild dog pile. I threw empty punches and twisted violently around and around like a terrorized tornado.

They continued to swarm around me relentlessly, and I could feel my adrenaline-laden body begin to succumb to fatigue. In my attempt to escape, I had somehow made my way to the four-foot-high fence, vaulted it, and crumpled to the ground. I looked up, and eight sets of empty, black wolf eyes peered back at me through the wire. I rose to my feet slowly and assessed the damage.

There I stood, in what had once been insulated heavy denim overalls, now shredded, bloodstained Daisy Duke shorts. My legs looked like hamburger and every puncture hole leaked a stream of red that now wove its way through the hair of my legs. I staggered to my truck. It was a forty-five-minute drive to the hospital, and I was all alone, with no phone. I needed to get there before I passed out from shock or loss of blood. My legs throbbed in pain the entire way, and I could feel my head getting lighter.

I pulled up at the emergency entrance of the Bozeman Deaconess Hospital and swung my car door open. My first step onto the pavement was excruciating, and as I stumbled toward the door, my boots sloshed with the blood that now filled them. A nurse greeted me at the door and asked me what happened. I remember the doubtful faces of the ER staff when I weakly uttered, "I was attacked by a pack of wolves." I know they thought I was crazy, or at the very least, delirious from the loss of blood. I was happy when I saw my regular doctor. He knew what I did for a living, and this wasn't the first time he had had to put a stitch in me, nor would it be the last.

I walked away from this experience with some valuable lessons, as well as a little post-traumatic stress. The biggest lesson of all was the recognition that I was hurt because of my own mistakes. The wolves were just being wolves. The shocking truth is that you can't learn anything the easy way. You have to immerse yourself deeply in order to understand anything deeply. This entails a great deal of risk when working with wild animals. The only way I could have learned something similar is if someone else had had my experience and relayed it to me. Even at that, you can never learn as comprehensively as I did without getting your instincts rocked the way I did that day. Many people have told me that a good animal person never gets bitten. I disagree. I feel that they are the ones who are not trying. You can have a relationship based on other people's experiences, but you can only take it to a certain level. My friend Dakota tore me apart that day, but I got back up, dusted myself off, and threw myself to the wolves again. I have been surrounded by wolves many times since then, but my actions were concise and accurate, and a product and result of my prior experience. I've never been bitten by a wolf again. Every day that I am on common ground with Brutus, it would be a mistake not to reflect back on that traumatic day with the wolves. Experience is key when it comes to working with animals, whether a wolf, a bear, or even a person. When I am around Brutus, I take all of my experiences collectively and apply them. I love every one of those moments, because without them, a relationship between man and bear would never be possible.

CHAPTER 8
FATHERS AND SONS

Y OU ONLY GET ONE CHANCE TO MAKE A FIRST IMPRESSION, but when it comes to a grizzly bear, you'd better hope the impression is a good one. I have been with several people during their first grizzly encounter, and the moment is always exhilarating and life-changing. To walk on common ground with an animal who is both noble and regal, and who can kill you in seconds, is not only very humbling but makes you realize how wonderful and wild the world is. It makes you feel alive. The people I have been with come from all walks of life: dentists, musicians, film producers, even my own family. Those who have had this unique experience have all learned their own personal life lessons from each encounter. Just a moment with or even a glimpse of a grizzly will have a profound effect on you. My dad's first encounter with a grizzly (or should I say grizzlies) is truly one for the ages. I gave him a phone call one afternoon, when I was in my late twenties, to see if he would like to come hike around one of my favorite spring-time grizzly viewing areas. In all his years of hiking thousands of miles in the wilderness, he had never actually seen a grizzly bear.

Dad met me the next day after driving down from Helena and we hopped into my truck and rode up a long washboard road. It was late in the day, so we decided to put most of our efforts into finding a spot to camp for the night. We found a nice one right along the river, complete with fire ring and leftover firewood from some college weekend gathering. We munched on habanero potato chips, sipped some cold beer, and listened to the roar of the river and the crackle of the fire. We reminisced about several wilderness adventures we'd had and laughed about our luck, and then complained about the rest of the world, as we usually did. As midnight approached, we tucked ourselves into our sleeping bags, eagerly antici-pating our hike.

We set out the next day before the sun rose, our head-lamps illuminating the trail ahead of us. It was a typical spring morning in Montana. The ground was still frozen from the cold night, making the soon-to-be-muddy trail easy to walk on. The robins celebrated with song the first hint of light on the horizon. The rising sun, which had already cast its rays on the great plains, was headed our way. I scanned the trail for tracks and signs as we walked up the steep path.

The morning breeze was brisk, and we could see our breath as our bodies warmed with the climb. Moose, elk, and coyote tracks overlapped the trail. The lack of grizzly tracks was to be expected this low on the mountain, but mostly I was pleased with the lack of boot tracks. I selfishly always get extra pleasure from a piece of wilderness unseen by the other goofy, two-legged, bald monkeys that make their way up here and usually scare everything away in an awkward attempt to walk in harmony in nature. Usually they fail miserably, missing the rhythm of the dance completely, stepping all over Mother Nature's toes, scaring away animals and leaving a trail of litter.

It's a dance we can all learn if we are willing to listen for the song and follow the steps that exist in our instincts and souls. Follow the lead of the animals. They are not walking around talking loudly. The moose are not listening to iPods or talking on their cell phones. There are plenty of playlists and conversations in the wilderness if you want to find them. If we can all just listen and look, and tread softly, our experience in the world will be more in balance and healthier. Most bear safety booklets or signs instruct individuals who are traveling in bear country to make noise in order to avoid bear/human conflict. The result is to scare the bears away and disturb everything else around. In that fashion, it does not seem like much of a wilderness experience to me. My recommendation is simple. If you are afraid of conflict with bears, go to the beach or the city park. If you want to hike in bear country, learn about them first and go with someone who can teach you to coexist with them.

As the sun began to peek over the eastern mountaintops,

the ground began to warm and the colors of spring began to erupt from the darkness. Glacier lilies, shooting stars, and penstemon glowed against the sage, mud, dry grass, and remaining snowdrifts. The air was fresh and clean; it smelled like the first spring that ever was.

I kept constant watch as we pushed further up the trail, now sweating under our warm coats. Now it was a duel of senses. Who would find whom first? A grizzly bear's sense of smell is seven times stronger than a bloodhound's. I needed to pay attention to the direction of the wind, constantly monitoring it and changing our heading to compensate, lest our scent betray us from miles away.

Ever since I was a young boy, I have been very keen on identifying animals by smell, slight glimpses, sounds, and by a sense that is hard to explain. I like to call it the sense of "life." I will often be walking or driving down the road, and then for some reason I'll stop, pick up my binoculars, and look in a direction behind me, to see an animal on a distant ridge, its head bobbing up and down, barely in sight. Though it's miles away and out of sight, smell, and hearing range, I feel it. It has happened over and over again, some primordial sense left over from being hunters or the hunted, one I have rediscovered and exercise regularly. It's a sensitivity to energy, though I get only hints of energy from wild animals in the distance. When it comes to Brutus or to people I know well, there is a wide variety of "flavors" of energy. Being attuned to these will help you determine how to interact. Whether it's Brutus or my wife, if I am not getting a good "vibe," I just leave them alone.

Something caught my senses and I looked over into the

deep sage to see a dark animal moving through. I watched it carefully to try to determine an outline. I grabbed my dad's sleeve and pulled him toward me to merge our outlines into one. As it lifted its head, it became obvious from its long ears and funny face that it was a cow moose. She put her head back down to graze and we tried to move past her on the tree line without disturbing her. Though grizzly bears were on my mind, you could never let your guard down, even when you were around a moose. I have had a couple of not-so-happy moose encounters. Like grizzly bears, mother moose are particularly defensive of their young. I encountered a cow moose and her calf on a trail when I was a teenager. She charged after me and I ran. She caught up to me quickly and was just about to stomp me into the ground when I dove off the trail into some thick bushes. There she stood, staring at me from the trail. I held still, scared out of my mind. She looked at me for a moment, realized I was not much of a threat, and went back to her calf. Others have not been so lucky. Several people have been killed in similar situations. I have also heard stories of moose chasing people and running them up a tree. The moose will stand patiently waiting at the tree's base for days. Mother moose are not only protective, they hold grudges, too.

As we went higher and higher, I started to notice the lack of hard-outlined tracks in the trail, and the new, subtle imprints of big toes here and there. Grizzly tracks. Fresh grizzly tracks only minutes before, the toes thawing the frozen frosty mud and its claws gently pecking the packed earth. We continued up the tree line, walking slower now. We were in the presence of something bigger and badder, and our senses were working overtime. I caught a movement in the distance and saw two dark spots moving in the meadow ahead. Two sub-adult grizzly bears dug frantically side by side in the icy shadows. We crept up a little closer and found a nice fallen tree to sit on.

The sun popped over the crest of the morning horizon, warming us with its glory as we sat comfortably and watched the two adolescents do their best to find their first meals of the year. My dad and I remained quiet, smiling at each other, sharing this peaceful wild moment together. My dad's first grizzly bear sighting!

We watched the two bears as they moved back and forth over the meadow, smelling for quarry under the ground. They would identify something beneath the ground, plant their noses against the mud, and begin digging. Using their noses as fulcrums, they would swivel around and dig in a circular fashion. When their heads were completely under the ground, my dad and I would whisper comments back and forth, and shift ourselves around to get more comfortable. Little did the four of us know that an interruption of this peaceful meadow was closing in rapidly like a dark cloud.

The young grizzly bears noticed the interruption first, their heads popping up from their holes simultaneously. I looked at my dad and checked the wind to make sure we were not the source of their unease. We weren't. One of the teens stood on its hind legs and looked down the meadow away from us, and then swiftly plopped to all fours and turned as if it was going to run in the opposite direction. They began to huff to indicate their dismay. Huffing is a sound that most bears make when they are uncomfortable, a repetitive blowing of air from their nose and mouth. They do it when they are frightened, angry, worried, or agitated. As the two youngsters continued to demonstrate their displeasure, I heard a third huffing sound coming from out of sight, down the slope of the meadow. Was it just an echo?

Like a hairy Mack truck on a mission to run over everything in its path, a large male grizzly walked swiftly into sight, on a quick beeline across the meadow toward his two fellow grizzlies. He had come to kick some ass, and he was strutting his stuff on the way to doing it. He walked with rigid legs, head held low, and was chomping his gigantic jaws together, the clacking of his teeth echoing through the meadow. The young bears had no interest in testing the big bear's machismo. They soon disappeared into the forest, leaving their meadow full of goodies to the new bear in town. The large male grizzly stopped and stood up to rub his back on a tree as a celebration and demonstration of his dominance. My heart pounded. I felt like it was time to run and hide, too. My dad and I sat perfectly still. The last thing we wanted this bully to know was that two even wimpier beings, and bald monkeys at that, were sitting on a log watching him gloat and scratch. The bear walked up and inspected all the excavations that the little bears had left behind but he was not terribly enthused. His interest seemed less in eating and more in teaching some snot-nosed cubs a lesson or two. He continued to follow the tracks of the scurrying adolescents. I couldn't help myself. I had to follow, too! I wasn't going to miss this bruiser putting on a clinic of grizzly power.

My dad looked at me as if I had lost my mind, and truth be told, I probably had, yet he reluctantly followed me, wrapped up in the thrill of the chase. I often make risky choices in the pursuit of witnessing something that will help me understand all wild things better. My father had two choices: to be with his crazy son and follow the action, or stay by himself, on a grizzly-saturated mountain. He would come to find out that afternoon that sitting alone in the sun would have been a much safer choice.

If there was any doubt that the grizzly thought he was a badass, we watched him walk through trees, literally. If there was a tree in his path that was less than six inches in diameter, he would walk right over it, knocking it over, and then piss on it as it passed through beneath him. This bear had a 'tude with a capital "T," and we were foolishly following him whereever he went!

The giant bruin moved up the meadow, which now was growing narrower and narrower. He came to the point where the meadow ended and vanished behind a snowdrift, and off into the forest out of sight. We crept forward, making sure not to get too far behind so we wouldn't miss anything and boy, were we in for a sight. Suddenly that same bear came straight toward us. He must have caught our scent and turned to follow us, and here we stood, like the two bears earlier in an open field. We scampered like two little squirrels toward the nearest stand of trees, a cluster of five tall Douglas firs. The first limbs were high, and my sixty-five-year-old father had no chance of getting up there on his own. With a grumpy testosterone-filled grizzly approaching, I boosted my dad just high enough that he could grab a limb and pull himself up. I ran to an adjacent tree, leapt like a frog full of rocket fuel, and climbed as fast as I could.

Mr. Grizzly couldn't have cared less about applying any more effort. I could tell he was amused by making us look like two chipmunks in a tree. It was a nice distraction from his harassing the other two bears, but the last thing he wanted was to waste more energy on the likes of us. Instead, to humiliate us more, he was just going to dig around and eat below the trees we now sat in, lounge in the sun if he liked, and mostly just enjoy torturing us, letting us know which species was dominant on this mountain. As we perched in the branches, we both were enjoying this up-close bird's-eye view, wondering all the while if we were going to be spending the night here. My dad was certainly having quite the grizzly "encounter"!

It was an uneasy feeling. I took advantage of this unique vantage point and popped off a few great photos. It was fascinating to literally sit above this grizzly and look down at the hole he was digging, watching his every move. I had never been this close to a grizzly bear. To me, this was like a front row seat to the greatest show on earth. The big bear found a spot that must have had some great reward below, because he really started digging in, flipping clods of dirt, making a dent in the earth in no time at all. He had now dug so deep that only the rear end of his six-hundred-pound body was visible.

Just then, from behind me, I heard a familiar noise. More grizzly huffing. I strained to turn and look, and to my surprise, just behind me on the ground, was *another* big male grizzly. He was big and mean, and had come to this meadow to do some bullying of his own. I threw pinecones at my dad to try to get his attention. He tried to turn but he couldn't because of the way he had situated himself on the limb. The new bear charged out toward the other bear's half-exposed rear end. He sprinted toward what he felt was a easy fight, but when he came to within about 15 yards, the massive grizzly revealed himself from his underground activity. The new bear couldn't put the brakes on fast enough. He had misjudged his foe and was now trying to get himself out of the situation as smoothly as possible. The big grizzly wasn't amused and, without a second thought, shot out of his hole like a bullet and raced after the bear who had made the wrong choice. The chase went off into the woods, out of sight. This time, it didn't take me long to realize that we had to get out of there while the getting was good.

We slid down the trees, gave a quick look around, and hiked briskly down the mountain. As we left the meadow, another grizzly appeared from the trees opposite us on the far side of the clearing. There were grizzlies everywhere! Unfortunately, we had had enough excitement for one morning, so we didn't stick around to enjoy them. We didn't say much until we got about halfway down. Then we recapped the entire morning about twenty times, laughing and shaking our heads, and trembling all over from leftover adrenaline. It was a great day, one we will never forget, and it comes to mind every time we walk back into grizzly country. It's this drug of untamed unpredictability and humiliation that mountain men become addicted to and that keeps us searching for more. It is this intoxication that has fueled my work with animals as a naturalist and conservationist. It is this very feeling that led me to Brutus, with whom I now have my very own father-son relationship.

I remember when I thought I was bigger and tougher than

my dad. I think that every man has gone through it. It usually happens at around age sixteen, when you're full of testosterone and now an inch taller than your old man. A disagreement will arise, and instead of submitting the way you usually do, you decide that you are a man now, you know everything, and you are going to give your father a lesson. Somehow it always ends the same way, as you sit there wishing you could hold some ice over your bruised ego, but you respect your dad about a thousand times more than you did ten minutes earlier. I remember when my own boy, Brutus, came of age. The only difference was, he was four years old and wighed about five hundred pounds, and could take me out with one punch. But I could never let him know it. That's when it became a case of mind over matter. Or should I say guts over instincts. What I needed, in those moments, was a good bluff.

Brutus and I had a father-son tussle at the sanctuary late one summer evening in 2006. I had just tossed a large chunk of frozen salmon into the pond for Brutus. He pulled the ten-pound slab out of the pond and settled in on the grass to nibble on it at his leisure. I left him to eat in peace, and went into the office and checked my messages. One message needed urgent attention and required that I drive into Bozeman as quickly as possible. This was a bit of a problem, because the only other employee on duty was not capable of bringing Brutus in for the night. So I had to go out and interrupt his evening meal and bring him inside to finish it, as state law requires that all the bears at the sanctuary stay in a secure building during the night.

As I approached him to grab his salmon to lure him in, he

spun around to confront me, with a sharp growl and a pouncing step in my direction. When he made his motion toward me, I was caught off guard and reacted by stepping back, a demonstration of submission, admitting I was wrong and that now he was in charge. In his mind he had won, and I had lost. He was right, and it wasn't going to be easy ground to make up. I suddenly knew that I had to counter-react, and in a decisive way. I needed to show him that *I* was still the father.

Like a freight train, I steamed toward Brutus with as mighty a roar as I could muster. I knew that I had to go full tilt and not let up no matter what happened. As I got within about 10 yards, he appeared to have no intentions of budging. I was playing chicken with a grizzly bear! I kept my focus and speed, and roared even louder. Just about a step before collision, Brutus jumped up and ran off, leaving his treat behind. Now was the time to gain some ground. I scooped the salmon up in one motion and chased him all over the sanctuary roaring. Taking it even a step further, I pulled down my pants with my other hand, pissed on one of the boulders, and proceeded to stomp around my regained "territory." Brutus watched sheepishly from a few feet away, eliminating any doubt that he knew who the boss was. I walked over to him, kindly now but firm, and then we walked calmly together into the denning kennels and I returned his salmon. He quickly resumed eating and I scratched his neck a bit before hurrying off. Our father-son relationship remains a key element of our bond. It is this mutual respect that allows me to remain safe. Animals are mentally healthy only when a hierarchy is in place. That is

how they function on a day-to-day basis. Without this struc-
ture, they feel chaotic and lost. In my effort to give Brutus
all he needs physically, mentally, and spiritually, this hierarchy is essential. It is not built on aggression or violence but
on love and respect. It comes from an emotional mutual
understanding that is deep and complicated. The synchro-
nization of two species takes time, but coexistence is possible.
I do not treat Brutus like a human, and I don't pretend to be
a bear. Instead, we respect each other for what we are, and
find a way to communicate when we are together.

My connection to Brutus is like a dance. Two beings of
different species understanding each other without speaking,
and often without sound. This rhythmic communication is
often very subtle body language, finely tuned from years of
observing and understanding one another. We have shared
the same language all along but we didn't know it in the
beginning. This took many misinterpretations, stepping on
each other's toes so to speak, and constant reassurances, as
with the salmon. But with time, and the willingness to dig
deep into my own animal instincts, it has again become my
nature, my true native tongue. This connection, or awareness
of something that has always existed, has allowed me to
understand nature at a different level, something I practice
every day with Brutus.

During the filming of *Expedition Grizzly* for National
Geographic Channel in 2008, I had over a hundred individual grizzly bear sightings in the Yellowstone region. Grizzlies are not known for their tolerance, and they maul a few
humans every year. Often this is the victim's first encounter
with a grizzly bear. I had some close encounters myself, but

with my ability to read an animal's intentions, I was able to make the right choices to avoid conflict. As I said before, first impressions count for a lot. This bridge from human to animal can help us understand animals better and to walk in sync with nature, but maybe more important, it helps us understand ourselves and those around us. As my relationship continues to mature with Brutus, it helps me understand my own parents. Being a father or mother isn't easy, if you can't understand your children for who they are. I respect my parents more than ever, and I truly enjoy my relationship with them now that we are all adults, and I look forward to my future with Brutus. The respect all people and things deserve was shown to me by the very respect and trust that has developed between me and Brutus.

CHAPTER 9
DANGEROUS ENCOUNTERS

IT WAS EARLY SPRING 2008. THOMAS WINSTON, LESLIE
Gaines, and Becker Holland had formed a production company called Grizzly Creek Films. The genesis of this company was the green light they had been given for the
television documentary *Exhibition Grizzly*. The documentary would follow me into the wilds of the Yellowstone
ecosystem in search of grizzly bears in their natural habitat.
Then, in both an educating and entertaining manner, I
would integrate Brutus into the show to put it all in perspective. It was an exciting time for all of us. We were all rookies
and we were all thrilled to have this opportunity, our first real
film project, and it was going to be for the prestigious

National Geographic Channel. The days were growing warmer and longer, which meant the grizzly bears would be coming out of their dens soon, some with new cubs in tow. So to play my part, I had to do what I do best, and that's track and find grizzly bears. With a lot of enthusiasm and quite a few butterflies in my stomach, it was time to get the expedition under way. I was full of pride when I opened the door to my truck, hopped in, and made the drive to Yellowstone National Park.

It was a typical spring morning in late April, and the snow had just begun to melt. My destination was a place a friend of mine had showed me years before, near Tower Junction, along the Yellowstone River. I arrived at the trailhead, anxious, full of zest, and ready to find some bears. As soon as I left the truck I was met with the typical spring obstacle course. I had to trudge through deep snow that was now melting in the heat of the sun, and the virtual oceans of mud that come with it.

As I walked through the snow, the weight of my body would break the icy and brittle surface and I would sink into the sludge. This happens every year. Until then, most of us have been sitting around all winter getting fat. On your first hike out, with the sun beating down on you, you climb on top of the snowdrifts and they seem to be holding your weight, and just when you think you're doing fine, the "floor" gives way and you find yourself post-holing up to your crotch, sweating in the heat, as you struggle to worm your way out.

After about twenty minutes of this, and truly exhausted, I finally made my way to a windswept ridge, where the wind had blown the snow off the top and what remaining snow was there had now turned to mud in the new spring sunshine. I could see that other animals were using the same path in the mud that I was. I could see the tracks of big horn sheep, wolves, deer, and elk, but I didn't see the familiar five-toed track of the grizzly bear. As I wandered up the ridge that closely hugged to the cliffs along the Yellowstone River, I walked directly into a herd of bighorn sheep. Neither of us was willing to go off the path, so I moved to one side of the trail and they obliged and moved to their side. They looked beautiful as they nibbled on fresh shoots of spring grass.

I walked further up the ridge, and as I wound through some Douglas firs some ravens suddenly flew up from the ground and landed in the treetops. I knew something was dead. And as I mentioned, wherever there is something dead there are grizzly bears. I edged forward to get a better look.

As I came over a rise, there ahead of me in the melting snow was a dead cow elk. The tracks of birds, coyotes, and even a lone wolf littered the snow around it. I moved forward a little more to investigate. The elk was mostly intact. What a wonderful prize for a bear this would be. I was disappointed not to see any grizzly tracks, so I moved on. I climbed higher on the ridge and looked down at the river. I found a nice little spot out of the wind, pressed my back against a log, and tried to catch some springtime rays while I waited.

The river roared as the snowpack melted. As I leaned against the log, some more bighorn sheep began to graze nearer. I sat back and enjoyed the show, and they got as close as five feet away, unthreatened by my lazy posture. Since this was one of the few areas in Yellowstone National Park that had cell phone service, I quickly began to take pictures with my phone, the only camera I had, to send to my wife, who loves to see wild images from my travels, especially when she is in hectic Los Angeles.

The smell of fresh dirt was in the air as the grass began to protrude from its winter-long sleep, and I could feel all of Yellowstone coming to life around me. After a long, cold winter, there's nothing better than sunshine, and everything in nature rejoices with happiness. At that moment, the grass, the bighorns, the river, and I grew stronger in the sun's rays. As I sat in my little piece of paradise, I noticed something walking along the river's edge. I lifted my binoculars and gazed down through the lenses at my first grizzly bear of the year. And, oh, what a grizzly bear it was.

It was a big male grizzly and this wasn't his first spring. He walked like a bear on a mission, in search of food and a mate. Not far along the river's edge, lying directly in his path, was a large bull bison, and I thought to myself that this was going to be interesting. Two of the most remarkable animals in the park's ecosystem were on a collision course. As the grizzly bear grew nearer to the robust beast, the bull bison made a charge. Though it was only a quick lurch in the bear's direction, its mere size made the bear stop quickly in its tracks. There they stood, face-to-face, each waiting for the other to make the next move. They both represented the finest of their species but they didn't get to old age by being stupid. They truly didn't want to mess with each other, and the conflict had no reward. The bison could be injured or killed and the energy the bear would exert far outweighed the potential injury he could receive from being gored by the bison. So they each ambled on their way, giving each other respectful glances.

As the large grizzly disappeared, I knew I had to get a better look. I didn't want to leave my warm little spot in the sun, but I had a documentary to make. I left the bighorn sheep behind and headed down a game trail that went toward the river. The trail was deeply worn from decades of animals crossing the river. It paralleled a deep wash and wound down deep through the pine trees. About a hundred yards in, a grizzly bear suddenly stepped out on the trail not more than six yards in front of me.

My heart seemed to stop as we stood there staring at each other. I could see in the grizzly bear's demeanor that he didn't want a bad day, just a meal and some time in the sun. I quickly moved my hand to the bear spray in my chest holster. With my thumb now on the trigger, I gently spoke to the young male bear: "Hey, buddy, I don't want a bad day either." After years and years of spending most of my days looking at bears, their body language is as familiar to me as my native tongue and I knew an easy resolution was possible.

He hung his head low and looked at me out of the corner of his eye. He was a young bear, and he didn't want any problems. We stood motionless for what seemed like an hour. It amazed me how relaxed I got. In fact, I wanted to document the moment, so I reached for my cell phone to try to snap another picture for my wife. But when I pushed the button to capture the photo, to my dismay it read MEMORY FULL from the countless photos I'd taken of the bighorn sheep. I frantically tried to erase them.

We were both waiting to see who was going to make the next move. He took a very slow start to his left just off the trail's edge. I copied his move exactly, taking a very slow step to my left. Again we stood motionless, like two cowboys on Main Street at high noon. We both had our hands on our pistols, but neither of us wanted to draw. Again he made the next move, another small step to the left, this time even slower. I again mimicked his move exactly. I continued to speak to him softly, and projected my intentions through my body language that this was a duel I wanted nothing to do with.

We continued to make small steps in a semicircle, never increasing the distance between us, to the point where we each ended up in the other's footsteps where we had stood at our first encounter. As soon as his paws landed back on the trail, he continued up it toward the ridge. I knew where he was going. With the wind in our face, I dialed Thomas and Leslie, my National Geographic producers, who were waiting in Bozeman, to tell them that I had a grizzly going toward an elk carcass and this was going to be some exceptionally great footage. I lagged back a bit so as not to follow too closely. As I crested the ridge, I watched the little bear settle in for his first meal of the year.

He had the entire carcass to himself, truly a spring bear's dream come true. The bear gorged himself, stripping off giant mouthfuls of meat. After eating for several minutes, he would take a break. The bear would walk to the ridge line, look around for competition, and then return to his stash. He continued eating, but soon his breaks became more frequent. He stopped checking for danger and took a nap on top of the carcass. As he lay there in the sun with a full belly, I thought to myself that I had rarely seen a happier, more content bear.

Life for a grizzly bear consists of really one thing, and that is finding its next meal. It is a minute-to-minute, day-after-day struggle. A grizzly bear is an opportunist, and when presented with the path of least resistance when it comes to feeding itself, it rarely turns away. Only in the most desperate of times will it throw all the rules out the door and try to add human to its menu.

It's hard to judge a person or an animal without meeting them. And I definitely will never judge a person solely on somebody else's interpretation. Whether it's in books, in the newspaper, or on television, you are only getting a slice of the story as interpreted through someone else's prejudice and bias. If you took all the footage that has been filmed of me in the field and gave it to the right person, they could edit it and make me look any way they wanted. I would hate to think that someone was judging me based on thirty minutes of subjectively spliced tape.

WHAT LITTLE I KNOW ABOUT TIMOTHY TREADWELL, BETTER known as the "The Grizzly Man," is from things that I've seen on television, books that I've read, and conversations that I've had with his friends, so I admit I am forming only a partial picture of him in my mind's eye. One thing is for certain: he was a very passionate man who was trying to do something good for the world. When I watched the documentaries and then learned of his death, my initial response was much the same as everyone's. Here was this man taking great risks, getting too close to bears, and from what I saw on the screen, he didn't know much about them or how to interact with them to both species' mutual comfort, safety, and benefit. He seemed very foolish and it seemed that it would certainly end badly. I remember that when I heard about his death, I said, "I told you so." But now that I know more, and actually have visited some of the same places that Timothy visited, I have a different perspective. Again, because I never got to know him, my perspective is probably only a fraction of the truth.

Timothy Treadwell spent thirteen years studying the coastal brown bears of Alaska. During those years, he lived peacefully among some of the largest bears on earth. He was clearly doing something right. Some people disapproved of his often anthropomorphic references to the bears, though when I visited the same areas, I couldn't help but think about the bears in much the same way.

The bears in Alaska are very different from any bear I've dealt with before in my own work. They are very docile, and their forgiving nature is unlike their Yellowstone cousins. I found myself becoming complacent and wanting the bears to be my "friends." In Yellowstone, the bears are not forgiving, and at the slightest sign of people, they usually run away, or, in a rare case, maul you. There is some speculation that the Yellowstone grizzly bear behaves this way because it was a plains animal. The grizzly bears' original range went all the way east nearly to the Mississippi River. This was a land abundant with things to eat and predators that liked to eat them. The grizzly had many enemies out on the plains, but it didn't have anywhere else to go. It couldn't run into the forest or over the mountain, so instead, it would fight to defend itself. It is common thought that this behavior carried on as we forced the grizzlies to the west and destroyed their habitat. So when faced with fight or flight, they often revert to their old ways and fight.

Had Treadwell gone to Yellowstone and exercised the same behavior that he did in Alaska, he might have been killed earlier. In Alaska, particularly in the protected areas where Treadwell hung out, the bears will approach you without fear, or else they ignore your presence. If anyone had spent as much time as he did around the same bears, I would bet that the majority of them would have ended up behaving the way they did with Treadwell. But we must all understand that it wasn't necessarily Treadwell's day-to-day behavior that got him into trouble. If anybody had been in the same situation as Treadwell and his girlfriend, Amie, they would likely have met the same fate. The mistake they made was that they did not take the proper precautions while living in grizzly country. An electric fence around their camp, bear spray, and recognition of certain behaviors—a basic working knowledge of bear language—would have saved their lives. Treadwell had carried bear spray in the past but felt it caused too much discomfort to the bears, so he had stopped using it. While I appreciate the idea of walking on equal ground with the bears, without any advantage, as the adaptive species it is *our* responsibility to protect the bears from us. Bear spray does exactly that. It teaches the bear that if it tries to harm us, it's not going to like the results, and therefore it learns and evolves a behavioral pattern not to attack. The bear that killed Timothy and Amie was hungry and desperate, a type that is rarely seen in coastal Alaska. A good part of why coastal Alaskan grizzlies are so easygoing is because of their comfortable lifestyle. They have abundant food and few enemies, and their personalities reflect this easy way of life. The bears that Treadwell got to know were all fat and happy, and he based a lot of his own behavior in Yellowstone on his interaction with contented Alaskan bears. He apparently let down his guard and also failed to recognize the signs of a desperate, hungry bear.

TREADWELL STAYED LONGER IN HIS FAVORITE AREA THAT year than he ever had before. It was late fall, a crucial time for bears as they try to fatten up for the long winter hibernation in their den. It is said that the bear that killed Timothy and Amie was an older bear who had likely had a poor summer and was having a hard time finding food that fall. When the bear encountered Timothy and Amie, he looked at them as protein. Nobody was there to see how they reacted to this bear's presence, so it's hard to speculate what, if any, mistake he made could have been the fatal one.

WHEN I AM IN GRIZZLY COUNTRY I RECOGNIZE THAT EVERY bear is different, and I react accordingly, never projecting the behavior of past bears on new ones. I always assess each bear's behavior and type in great detail before making any decision about my own behavior. My recognition of each bear's personality, intentions, and overall demeanor comes from years and years of observation and close interaction with grizzlies. It is not an exact science, and when I am in the field there is always a certain amount of risk. You must pick and choose your situations and always err on the side of caution to keep the odds in your favor. In my case it's a very calculated risk, one that I am not afraid to back out of at any sign of potential peril. In the end, even if it's my mistake, the bear will pay the price with its life, and that is the last thing that I would ever want. My backup plan in a situation that is out of control is bear pepper spray. Though it is miserable for the bear for an hour or so, it's better than the loss of its life or mine, and again, it provides an opportunity for the bear to learn and evolve and adapt a bit of its behavior. I truly believe that Timothy Treadwell felt the same way about bears dying, but unfortunately many bears paid the price with their lives for killing and/or eating him and his girlfriend. Quite simply, if Treadwell had had bear spray that day, he and his girlfriend would likely be alive, and so would all of the bears who attacked them.

Though in some way I will continue to always live in his shadow, and apologize for his mistakes, I feel like it is part of my responsibility to show the world that with much vigilance, experience, and respectable behavior that a coexistence with grizzly bears can be done safely and that what I am doing is not harebrained.

I will continue to try to counter the public's skewed perception of the Treadwell incident and hope that people will understand what really happened and how it could have been prevented, and learn not to fear the grizzly bear. Nature can be savage, and the thing we can do for ourselves and the world is to learn from such moments.

It was during the filming of *Expedition Grizzly* that I faced my first desperate bear. There wasn't a cloud in the sky. The sun had just begun to light up the sky, casting streaks of pink, periwinkle, and baby blue across the freshly snow-dusted landscape. The frosty birds welcomed the rising sun with song. Tom, the producer/director of photography, and I had gobbled our breakfast during our sleepy ten-minute drive from the tents at the campground up to the trailhead. We tried to warm ourselves with coffee made the night before and left for us in a thermos along with two hard-boiled eggs and two cups of strawberry yogurt. I managed to scarf it all down with both hands by driving with my knees most of the way. Small blobs of yogurt and drips of coffee flecked my jacket thanks to potholes and curves in the road.

Our destination wasn't an official trail but a park service road to an electrical substation hidden from the view of the tourists. We parked along the service road in front of the locked gate and managed to catch some warmth from the truck's heater, which had just kicked in. Then we put on our gators, grabbed our binoculars and bear spray, and strapped on our heavy backpacks loaded with camera gear.

We had more buckles, straps, and laces than a woman's shoe store, but it was all part of the tools essential to good wildlife filmmaking. As we made our way down the road, I looked eagerly at the new snow for fresh tracks. It was all going to melt soon in the warming daylight, so I needed to get on the trail of a grizzly as soon as I could. As we rounded a bend and walked over a rise, we stared into a vast valley of sage with a meandering river running through it. We call it "the hole." The scene was monochromatic, dusty green and white, speckled with the amber coats of sporadic elk grazing. Grass-eating animals don't move much. They find a good spot, eat for a minute or two, lift their heads here and there checking for danger, eat some more, and then take a few steps in one direction or other and start over again. I was looking for fast-moving specks. These specks are the beasts who eat the grass eaters.

My eyes are calibrated to home in on these movements and to watch the grass eaters for deviations in their benign behavior that might tip off a predator. It didn't take me long to find one. A big brown dot was moving quickly across the virtually motionless scape. The elks' ears, eyes, and noses pointed toward the bear like weather vanes cutting into a cold, ominous wind. It was a big male grizzly, and he was on a mission, moving in the direction of the cow elk. The grizzly was doing a behavior called bird-dogging. Just like a bird dog on the hunt to flush out a pheasant, this bear weaved back and forth with his nose to the ground looking for his own quarry to jump.

I watch the big male grizzly zigzagging rapidly through the sagebrush and snow, looking for something to eat. His gait was somewhere between a walk and a jog. He appeared desperate, his movement was frenzied, acting on a height-ened level of need. I looked through my binoculars as he stopped and stared in our direction. Through the power of my lenses, I locked eyes with him and found myself looking into the face of a bear that I didn't like the looks of in the least. His hipbones jutted out through his mottled and unhealthy hide. His eyes sat deep in his skull, and his jowls hung low and had strings of saliva drooling off them. His mouth gaped open, showing old worn-down yellow teeth. He strained to look at us—we must have looked like two small bumps out on a sagebrush plain. In his mind, we were two small meals only five hundred yards away. He came toward us like a heat-seeking missile.

With a 35-mile-per-hour wind gusting in our face, I lost sight of the slather-faced giant in the topography as he made a beeline for us. There was no hope of his smelling us with this wind, and, maybe more of concern, we would probably spray ourselves in the face if we used our bear pepper spray. When the grizzly reappeared in our line of sight, he was less than a hundred yards away, still moving in a straight line directly toward us at a quick pace. He had moved within a dangerous distance of us, so now it was time to blow our cover and for me to identify myself as a human and scare him away. I hate scaring bears—it is against every fiber of my being—but I have done it a few times as a last resort when they are getting too close.

I stood up, waved my arms, and simply said, "Hey, bear!" in a loud, strong voice. Well, this didn't have the results I was hoping for, as the bear lowered his head and started gaining speed. I thought he must not have heard me in the turbid wind, so I shouted again, this time even louder, waving my arms like crazy. The results were the same, adrenaline rushed through me, and my mind went into emergency mode. I looked over at Tom and said, "Close your eyes and hold your breath, we are about to get f****ed up." I gave these instructions because I was going to step forward into the bear's path and try to deploy my bear spray into the hurricane of wind. We were certainly going to be sprayed, too, but maybe I could direct some of the spray toward the bear and distract him slightly from his attack. At the last second, when the bear was fifteen yards from us, I reached over and lifted my large backpack over my head. My intentions were to throw it in his path to give me an additional second to spray him. I yelled "Hey, bear!!" and he stopped ten yards away and stood up on his hind legs.

A long moment passed, as we stood face-to-face considering our next moves. I felt my heart pounding in my chest. There was nothing in the world at this moment but me and this monster of a bear, and a desperately hungry one at that. His eyes were dark, but even in my fear, I could see a soul in his expression. We shared our souls for a moment, just two beings in the vast universe. With my backpack as a hat, I was now as tall as he was, and I could see he was sizing me up. I held my position, and continued the charade. He gave my new stature another consideration and then dropped down to all fours and walked away. The next thing I heard was Tom exclaiming, "Holy Shit," and I agreed.

In the desperation of the moment, that bear was more than happy to eat two six-foot-tall human beings. He had thrown all the rules aside because he was now in survival mode. He had to feed himself to live. Grizzlies will run away at the first sign of a person most of the time, but when times are extremely tough, they have no other choice but to make an exception. We were three hundred pounds of protein, and in his mind it was his only option. But when one of those humans held his ground and suddenly became eight feet tall, it was just enough to change his mind. Tom and I were glad he did. It's funny when I realize how close that was, and how it was a simple matter of seconds and a last-minute reaction that prevented us all from having a bad day.

This was the same type of bear that killed Timothy Treadwell and his girlfriend, Amie Huguenard. A bear who was on his last legs, a hopeless creature in the struggle for life. This is where hard lines are drawn in brutal nature. These are the lines that we as humans have little control over and often not enough respect for. Most of us hide behind the walls of our homes and forget that these lines exist.

People like Treadwell walked close to the line often. I walk close to the line often. It's a place to feel what it truly is to be a member of the species Homo sapiens. It invokes a primordial effervescence. It's truly intoxicating, the feeling of being alive. To walk on common ground with an animal that can kill and eat people is humbling. Your mind is not loud with the thoughts and confusion of society. It's clear and silent, it's meditation at its fullest. It's an enlightened place where you will find out more about yourself than anywhere else. For those of us who have experienced it, it becomes our church, a place where you can clearly communicate with God. It's where I find my spirituality.

Brutus stands nearly 8 feet tall and weighs over 900 pounds.

Two big bears battle at Brooks Falls.

High on the talus slopes outside Yellowstone National Park.

A sow teaches her cubs the art of the "perfect catch."

TOP: *Jake, a friend of Brutus's at the Grizzly Encounter, investigates a snow man made by a local school group at the sanctuary.* BOTTOM: *"High Fives": Brutus reaches to give Casey a high five.*

ABOVE: *Brutus's 8th birthday celebration included a salmon piñata.*
OPPOSITE: *Brutus enjoys a good neck rub from Casey.*

Casey and Missi look on as Brutus devours his 8th birthday cake.

Brutus exits his den at Montana Grizzly Encounter.

Brutus shakes it off after failing his first solo fishing trip.

TOP: *Brutus takes a break from fishing with dad to show off to the camera.*
BOTTOM: *Brutus gets close, enjoying the spotlight.*

TOP: *Casey reels a fake fish through a trout pond to entice Brutus to fish.*
BOTTOM: *More showing off!*

Casey educating kids about grizzly bear conservation at Montana Grizzly Encounter.

Casey teaches Brutus the "pouncing" fishing technique at The Talking Hotdog Ranch.

A sow grizzly catches a salmon in midair atop Brooks Falls.

Brown bears gather at world-famous Brooks Falls in Katmai National Park, Alaska.

The animals who live it every day also find their spirituality here, and while we walk through their place of worship, we also must respect them and their faithful practices. We must look to them for lessons, for they walk through this sacred, wild temple in grace as we stumble around, interrupting its beautiful sermon.

CHAPTER **10**
ANTLER RIDGE

MAKING A WILDLIFE DOCUMENTARY CAN ONLY BE DONE well if you assemble a perfect team from the office to the field. But being in the field, on foot, requires a special level of trust and efficiency and a well-orchestrated team. I thought of my team as the tracking trio.

Thomas Winston, Rick Smith, and I downed our coffee and rubbed our eyes as we made our way toward the trailhead long before the sun began to rise. Like waking from hibernation, we stretched and groaned as we exited the truck. Strapping on our headlamps and our sixty-pound backpacks, we stared toward the moonlit skyline at our projected destination. We started making our way along the trail and gained elevation as the sun began to rise. The cold of darkness had frozen the soggy spring thaw, and our boots crunched the frozen mud and our breath exited as steam into the cold morning air. The trail snaked toward a bench where three large bison bulls were now also just waking up. Just before we reached the mammoth bovines, a thunder of hooves erupted off to our right, and like comets across the prairie a herd of pronghorn sped by only about thirty yards ahead of us. To see them sprinting at full speed, nearly 70 miles per hour, and so close at hand, was amazing.

As we moved up the crusty trail, we figured it was our very presence that had caused them to run. The three of us walked off the edge of the trail and gave the bison bulls a wide berth, expecting that they could be as grumpy as we were with this early-morning wake-up call. As the lights of the new day danced across the landscape below, we stopped to take in the breathtaking view. As awe-inspiring and spectacular as it was, we couldn't help but notice the gathering of cars near the trailhead we had left behind. At this hour in the morning, only wildlife filmmakers, seasoned wildlife viewers, and crazy people scurry through Yellowstone. I looked down through my binoculars to see what all the fuss was about. That's when I noticed that Bob Landis's white Subaru had pulled off the road.

Bob is a seasoned wildlife filmmaker who has captured some of the most astonishing wildlife moments ever. Several of his films are my favorite National Geographic specials. So if Bob was stopping, it was something worth looking at. We scanned the landscape for signs of wildlife, but we could not see anything out of the ordinary. Looking through my lenses, I saw nothing but wildlife viewers, sagebrush, and frosty grass. All at once, to our immediate left, a lone black wolf scampered toward us, his pack in tow.

This was our first day out together as a team, and although we are a well-oiled machine now, that day we awkwardly scrambled to assemble our gear to get the shot. I was carrying the camera in my backpack, Thomas had the tripod in his, and Rick the sound equipment. Now it was time to frantically put the puzzle together and be true National Geographic filmmakers.

Our frozen fingers fumbled as we tried to keep our eyes on the wolves while also keeping our minds on our task. Just as we got it all together, the entire pack had passed us and disappeared over the horizon. We wondered what it must've looked like from down below, three rookies looking for wolves, having them run right to us, floundering around like fish out of water, and then missing the entire shot. My guess is that Bob was not very impressed. Like children, we remained inspired by the encounter, and, unlike Bob, we were spry young men who were tough enough to follow all those wolves.

As we marched up the hill, the frozen grass began to thaw. On the north faces, snowdrifts still clung to the mountain. In the cold early morning, these temporary glaciers act as interstate highways; the hard-packed surface makes for swift travel. But as the day grows warmer, they turn into a treacherous form of quicksand. As we started up the ridge line, we could see the that wolves had already gained a mile on us, but we continued to climb the ridge with a degree of optimism. As promised, the temperature began to rise. Our bodies were out of shape from a winter of relative inactivity, and slowly began to suffer. Our backpacks seemed to get heavier and heavier, and then the warming snow became a pitfall. It's similar to walking down a sidewalk only to find that one section of concrete hasn't set completely and suddenly you're sinking into the earth. After struggling to get out, you manage to find another firm piece of sidewalk, carefully walk on it just enough to build confidence, and then sink up to your waist.

We remained determined, however, despite the fact that this merciless pattern happened over and over again. We were completely exhausted. We would all have just fallen over and tumbled down the hill if we hadn't been anchored by three feet of snow. And if that weren't enough, the icy crust on the surface of the snow sliced into our shins every time we stepped through the firm layer.

The pain and exhaustion were psychologically debilitating, on top of the fact that we were already humbled by losing the shot in the first place, but our rookie spirits kept us going. As we reached the refuge of barren ground, we all stopped to rest. I scanned the surrounding ridges for signs of life. I knew that bears faced the same obstacles we did, so I paid particular attention to the open barren meadows devoid of the daunting snowdrifts.

A familiar flash of movement caught my eye. As I pulled the focus of my binoculars, I laid my eyes on a grizzly bear. Like a kid singing a nursery rhyme jingle, I chanted, "I see a grizzly bear!" with a huge grin on my face. This was the first time Rick had spent any time with me in the wilderness, and I remember him laughing at me for my apparent youthful excitement. A deep valley lay between us and the bear, although the ridges that we both stood on met about three miles up at the head of the drainage.

We have two rules as filmmakers: if you see a grizzly, move toward it, and if you gain elevation, don't lose it. So we put these two rules into effect and decided to follow our ridge over to the bear's ridge. Then we would try to make our way down, sneaking into filming distance of the bear. As we made our way to the head of the valley, we noticed the wolves miles away, little specks disappearing into the vast openness of Yellowstone. It amazed us that they had so much endurance, even in the deep snow, leaving our ragtag pack of three in the dust.

After an hour of hauling our heavy packs higher and higher, we were thankful when our ridge connected with the other one. The new ridge was spectacular. Wildflowers jutted through new shoots of grass, and the hillside glistened with the reflection of the sun off decades of the antlers of fallen elk. In every direction as far as the eye could see, antlers littered the ground. It was truly one of the most amazing natural vistas I'd ever seen. And standing at nearly nine thousand feet elevation, it was hard to imagine the weather conditions of this location during the time the elk shed their antlers. Bull elk lose their antlers annually, usually in the month of March. During that time on this hillside, the snow had to be exceptionally deep and the wind had to be extremely frigid. The wind must have swept spots of snow away, and these giant bull elk had to have made their way through deep snow to get to those places. High on these windswept ridges, as these "kings" grazed on dried grasses, their crowns would fall next to the fallen crowns of other kings. Judging by the similar characteristics of some of the antlers, it looked like the same bulls had returned year after year to that location to shed their antlers. What was already a spectacularly beautiful landscape was made surreal by their presence.

The grizzly had gone from sight, so we blindly navigated our way toward where we had last seen it. The wind blew in our faces, but as the sun rose higher in the sky it warmed the earth. The ground began to thaw, the birds began to sing, and the smile of the sun played its narcoleptic trick on us. We sat down on the ridge, and soon we were all taking a springtime nap. I remember waking and looking around and realizing how ridiculously stupid it was to be napping on a ridge with a grizzly bear (and a pack of wolves) not far away. I woke the others, and we gathered our equipment and crept down the hill to where we hoped that bear would be.

The topography of the ridge formed natural blind spots, so I would peek over and around each hump to see what was around the corner. As we slowly stalked the unknown, anxiety and tension built within us. We knew we were getting closer, but didn't know how close. This was Rick's first time tracking grizzlies. He followed loyally, but I can only imagine what must've been running through his mind, following this young, seemingly insane guy through Yellowstone, chasing grizzlies.

As I slowly lifted my sight line over the next blind spot, to my dismay the first thing I saw were two fuzzy bear ears. Out of habit, my tracking and hunting experience caused me to drop quickly to the ground, to get out of sight line and hearing range. I scurried back to try and utilize the topography to hide. It was my hope that we could quickly set up and capture some footage of the bear as she rounded the corner toward us. I remember Rick's face as my slow, methodical steps turned into a quick retreating gallop. His dam of anxiety broke, and in fight-or-flight fashion, he took off like a gazelle. I remember whispering sternly, "No, no, no, no," as a frantic flight would only encourage the bear to chase him. He listened and halted, and we tried to set up the camera gear to film the bear.

We waited and waited and the bear never appeared. The last thing any of us wanted to do was retrace our steps and peek over the hill again, so we waited for a little while, and then impatience overtook logic, and I peered back over the hill again. This time the sow grizzly was a quarter mile down the hill. This was a nice distance to start at, so we filmed her grazing grasses and digging roots in the beautiful setting of the fallen elk antlers and fresh wildflowers. The wind direction was still in our favor, so we pushed in closer and followed her down the ridge step by step. Soon she vanished over another small hill, so we climbed to the top of an adjacent hill to look down and see where she'd gone, but she'd disappeared again.

Just down the hill, near a medium-sized mountain stream, I could see the remnants of an elk, who had most likely been felled by the winter scarcity. And I know that where there is a carcass, there is usually a bear. This was going to make a great sequence for our film. The meadow was deep in sagebrush and covered with large granite boulders. As we crept closer to the elk carcass, I stood atop the boulders to get a better view. I still could not see the grizzly but I knew she must have been near the food source.

The closer we got, the more I would check on her location. Now we were getting pretty close, and there was still no sign of her. I'd come to the realization that she likely smelled us and ran away. Dropping my guard and increasing my speed, I thought we would just walk to the elk carcass and do a great standup about elk carcasses instead. Certainly there would be some grizzly bear sign around it and would add a great element to the story, whether or not she showed up again.

About thirty-five yards from the carcass, I realized I had made a hasty decision. Erupting from the sagebrush, at very close proximity, there she stood. I almost dropped down again to hide, but I realized that my cover had been blown. I turned to my crew and found myself looking into the saucer-sized eyes of poor Rick. Luckily for us, the bear was as afraid as we were. She turned and sprinted away to the sagebrush, leaving nothing but flying mud in her wake.

It's in moments like those that you learn a valuable lesson, and our team learned an important one that day that played out right before our eyes. Patience is a virtue, and it can mean the difference between getting good footage and getting mauled by a grizzly bear. Our impatience had ruined a much-needed meal for the bear. The lessons learned that day would be utilized on future filming missions.

We headed back toward the truck, and during the entire trip down the mountain, we laughed as we recapped the story, talking over each other in elation. It's these shared moments that fuel our passion and keep us going back for more adventures, despite an occasional unproductive day.

The humility one feels in the presence of grizzlies is equal parts fear and joy. The bear had shaken our souls and knocked off the dust of monotonous modern life. We were born again, as fresh as our first day, feeling the energy of all things. We were alive. There are very few things that can evoke this emotion, but the grizzly bear can. It's part of what makes this animal so wonderful and so essential to our life. When the sun disappeared behind the hills, the day had ended for most, but not for us. We continued to bask in our happiness, which renewed our passion and goal to portray these incredible creatures as they really are: noble, wild, and an integral facet of our natural world.

CHAPTER **11**

MOUNTAIN MIGRATION

W HEN THE AVERAGE PERSON THINKS OF A GRIZZLY BEAR, they see an image of a bear standing in lush, tall, green grass alongside a river chock-full of salmon. The gluttons pick the ten-pound sockeye salmon from the water and gorge themselves. Seagulls dance on the breeze above their heads waiting to pick up the hefty leftovers. This typical image comes from years of wildlife documentary makers utilizing the Alaska coastal region for grizzly bear film locations. Most of the grizzlies on postcards, television shows, and magazine covers, are captured in this "bear paradise." Though Yellowstone sits thousands of miles to the south, I often see Alaskan coastal grizzly bears labeled as Yellowstone Park grizzlies. The Yellowstone region in Wyoming gets less than 14 inches of precipitation annually. It is truly a semi-arid desert. Plants and animals that you would expect to see in Arizona, such as jackrabbits, prickly pear cactus, rattlesnakes, and yucca, share a habitat with the Yellowstone grizzly. In fact, I find that Yellowstone grizzly bears and sagebrush go hand in hand. It's a world away from the Alaskan coastal waterways. To the east of the park stands the powerful Absaroka mountain range. It runs hundreds of miles, from Livingston, Montana, to deep into Wyoming. This mountain range is rugged and unforgiving, and high above its pristine wilderness valleys, punching through the clouds, are barren, jagged peaks made of mostly rock and ice. Few plants inhabit the top of this range, as constant high winds blow away almost anything that attempts to dig its roots in. A few sparse and robust species of wildflowers cling to the rocky cracks. These little flowers stand barely an inch high, and if they were any taller, they would surely disappear in the next gust of wind. They likely arrived as seeds riding a torrent, the same force that threatens to remove them from the mountain. There they spend a short period of time in the sun, as snow covers them for about ten months a year. When they are freed from their icy tomb they do not hesitate to flaunt their vibrant beauty. In a usually monochromatic landscape, suddenly the rocks and ice are now woven with bright pastel flowers in the shadows of the voids and fissures. Swaying in the wind, they are safe for a short time in this otherwise hostile environment.

As the days become longer, a winged midnight migration begins. From hundreds of miles away, lifting off from the great plains, bands of army cutworm moths leave the agricultural fields of wheat and alfalfa and take to the air toward Yellowstone country. Only about a dozen of the thousand peaks have the right ingredients to facilitate these new arrivals. Temperature, wind directions, and wildflower saturation all play a part in this intricate formula that determines these very select peaks. As the moths fly and are lifted and thrown about in the wild wind currents, they soon start depositing themselves high above the tree line of the Absarokas. In the heat of the day they nestle themselves deep into the rocks, but as the temperature falls at night, they emerge to gorge themselves on the nutritious nectar of the tough little wildflowers. High on these peaks they are virtually safe from all danger, enjoying the only food source in the area that they have all to themselves. But from the west, another migration begins, this time on foot.

As the valleys below grow hotter in the July sun, grizzly bears begin, one by one, to remember a special but desolate place that their mother showed them. The bruins trek upward out of the trees, and become mountaineers in search of food. It's not the nectar of wildflowers that interests them but those moths who have now arrived in the millions, blissfully gorging on unmolested nectar.

As the sun lifts above the horizon, the last of the midnight-feeding moths bury themselves deep in the chasms of the cool rock. There they wait for the return of the night, often by the thousands. Sheltered by half-ton rocks, they would seem to be worry-free. But with one swift swipe of a paw, a boulder is turned over, and then with quick flicks of the tongue, the grizzly bear laps up the moths that are exposed. Contrary to a common but misguided impression, bears are actually very dainty eaters. They almost never take oversized bites, and they make sure their food is clean and contains no debris or dirt. In the case of the moths, they literally eat them one by one. A flick of their sticky tongue can reward them with an occasional multimoth surprise, but they usually enjoy every succulent little moth-morsel one at a time. I have watched Brutus do this over and over. For example, if I emptied a bag of Skittles onto the ground, he would use his sticky tongue like an anteater to pick them up one at a time sometimes even avoiding his least favorite flavor, the red ones, until the end.

This grouping of bears up above the tree line only happens for a few weeks each year, which is why my own migration for documentation begins there. I prepare for this outing as if I'm about to climb Mount Everest. My backpack is loaded with ice axes, crampons, climbing gear, and other high-altitude mountaineering equipment. Of all of my annual trips in search of grizzly bears, this is certainly the most challenging.

My favorite vantage point from which to view the bears is Francs Peak, the highest in the Absaroka range, situating itself at over 13,000 feet. If I were out of shape at this time of year, it would mean missing this trek, and thus it's an impetus to continue hiking during the winter months!

After a long and bone-jarring trip several miles down a long dirt road that climbs steeply into the foothills, we parked and began our week-long filming expedition. This meant adding another couple of hundred pounds of camera gear to the already strenuous nature of the trek. On this particular trip we had a crew of eight: Josh, a local guy who knows the area like the back of his hand, to serve as a guide and navigator; Rick, Thomas, and I, who are the core film team; two producers, who would be base camp support; and two extra-strong mountain guys from Cody to help pack all the gear in.

Our first camp (base camp) was in a gorgeous mountain valley on the northeast side of the mountain. The valley was mostly without trees and lower down was filled with wild grasses and sedges. As we pushed our overloaded bodies to ever-higher altitudes and over the rolling emerald hills, we encountered large herds of elk taking advantage of the lush grass and the cool temperature. Finally the valley dead-ended in a head wall of rock, marking the lower reaches of the peak. Just below the cliffs and sheets of ice was a nice grassy bench, the perfect place to set up base camp. We erected a small tent city, and after a hearty meal tucked our-selves in for the night. We had to rest up for a predawn climb with heavy packs.

The morning temperature was below freezing, something we had forgotten about in mid-July. We quickly gulped down our hot coffee and devoured a simple breakfast. We slung our packs on our shoulders and picked our way out of the valley, weaving through an initial boulder field to the base of our first big challenge. There we stood looking up an extremely steep ice field that cut its way 500 feet in elevation on the north face of the peak. We took off our packs, sat on the icy rocks, and attached crampons to our boots. Our packs weighed well over 50 pounds apiece, and a slip anywhere on this glacier would surely have meant a slide that ended in a deadly crash onto the rocks below.

Each step had to be well-placed and double-checked with sharp kicks. One by one, step by step, we made our way precariously up the ice field. There were moments when we'd slip a little bit and get quite an adrenaline rush. Or we'd stand up too straight and the weight of our backpacks would almost pull us backward right off the mountain. And if my life weren't valuable enough, in my pack was a $120 thousand camera that I was responsible for.

At the top of the ice field, we suddenly encountered crumbling rock, and we sighed with relief. Even though we were only about a quarter of the way to our destination, the rock felt safer than the ice. But there were plenty of hazards lying ahead. The wind from here on out would gust up to 50 miles an hour and never let up. In this arid land the wind sucked any moisture out of your body, causing your skin to crack and your already dehydrated tissues to dry out even quicker. We were turning into ice-cold jerky. I still marvel at how the bears make this journey annually without breaking a sweat.

As we trudged forward, the lack of oxygen started to become more and more apparent. I always hit an energy wall at 12,000 feet, and without acclimating ourselves, each step with the heavy packs was that much more exhausting. The potential to capture a rare natural event on film motivated us to push on. The footing was sketchy and the wind continued to pound us. We'd stop often to catch our breath but never seemed to get a full intake, as the whipping winds would suck it right out of our lungs. We hugged the rocky ridge that made its way toward the summit. I scanned the talus looking for "boulders" of fur among the millions of boulders of rock. It was hard to believe but I knew there were grizzly bears somewhere in this lunar landscape. We continued our way through the unstable obstacle course of stone, now extravigilant as we rounded corners, knowing that a bear could be there. From time to time I would stop on the ridge to give the rough contours a glance for signs of life.

AS IF BEING IN CLOSE PROXIMITY TO DOZENS OF GRIZZLY bears wasn't enough, the wind would knock me from my feet and slam me to the sharp rocks just when I had started to relax. I would stand up, dust myself off, and move on slowly, my head constantly swiveling as I watched for bears. There was not much cover to conceal ourselves, just the topography of the mountain. The gusting wind benefited us now, as it would be difficult for the grizzly bears to smell us, our scent being swept away swiftly in the turbid air.

I will never forget when I saw them. We hiked over a small rise, and there below on a plain of rock and dust, six grizzly bears tirelessly worked through the boulders, like big hairy men in a quarry. The chinks and clangs of rocks echoed against the cliffs as boulders tumbled down and the bears quarried for moths. I sat in awe of the spectacle. I had never seen so many Yellowstone bears at once, and certainly not this close to each other. I thought this type of congregation only happened in the salmon-rich streams of

Alaska, or in the folklore of mountain men of the past. I knew I was witnessing something very extraordinary. Very few people have ever seen a grizzly bear. As many as 90 percent of Montanans have not. Though Montana is home to more grizzly bears than any of the other lower forty-eight states, most of its human inhabitants never get far enough from the road to see their official state animal. To see a half dozen Yellowstone grizzly bears at once is extremely rare. When faced with the raw beauty of pure nature before me, lacking any evidence of man, I find myself lost in its splendor, and it makes me feel like a child. It's moments like this that keep me believing in all that is good. And the untainted, honest harmony of rock and bear was complete perfection. There is no deceit on the mountain where I stood. The only thing that was uncertain was my footing.

When the opportunity presents itself, grizzly bears will congregate for a food source, like that day up on the mountaintop. In the Yellowstone region today this rarely happens. Mountain men and explorers left descriptions in some of their journals of extraordinary grizzly congregations. When herds of bison and other ungulates still roamed the land, it wasn't much different from what you see in the modern-day Serengeti Plain in north-central Tanzania in Africa. Massive migrations would happen, and when it came time for the herds to ford rivers, it often led to drownings. When these carcasses floated downriver, several would get jammed up on river banks, creating a massive food opportunity for the bears. At that time, dozens of bears would come together to take advantage of the situation, just like at the moth sites. I theorize that a great part of the steep decline in the grizzly bear population over the last century comes from the lack of these "congregated feeding" events. The feedings created an opportunity for males and females to come together during the mating season, resulting in a much higher percentage of females with cubs come springtime.

Another unique dynamic of these congregations is the formation of a temporary social hierarchy. I have worked in the captive-bear world in some aspect since 1994, so I got familiar with this dynamic due to the "forced" congregation of captive bears. It always amazed me. Here is a relatively solitary animal presented with a social situation. Bears will always work it out, and then develop it into something deeper. I have seen cliques form, I have seen temporary alliances, I have seen hatred, and I have seen lifelong love affairs. It's like a season of *Survivor*. The bears get to know each other very personally. And in their long life spans (up to thirty years in the wild), they remember their fellow bears, and deep relationships develop. Mothers with cubs turn boulders next to each other like lifelong gal pals. The cubs stand close to their mothers and stare across at the neighbor cubs. The sows work diligently and pay no attention to the other bears. The likely reason is that the two sows were once cubs standing together on this same mountain. They know each other and have developed a trust and understanding. A temporary hierarchy forms when two strangers meet on the slopes, but look deeper and you will find a long-standing set of social relationships that have blossomed over the decades.

Brutus has many beings in his life. Whether it's people, other bears, or even a dog, he has developed very distinct relationships with each which are constantly evolving. From time to time he is presented with a new potential relationship partner, and just like any of us, he takes time to get to know each of them. When it comes to bear-to-bear relationships, the learning curve is often quick and concise. They speak the same language and can communicate with brawn and power—not violence, but strength. When two bears come together for the first time, they exchange many intricate poses and subtle gestures. And when a human and bear come together for the first time, it happens exactly the same way, but the problem is that most humans do not recognize this type of communication. At that point confusion ensues, and misunderstanding can lead to a rupture in the relationship.

One of my close friends, Steve McMorran, whom we call Silvertip, decided one day to take his relationship with Brutus to the next level. I had worked for Steve in the beginning of my career at the Montana Fish Wildlife and Parks animal rehabilitation center in Helena. Steve took me under his wing and taught me a great deal of what I know about animal husbandry, capture, and emergency medical care. When I began the project of building Montana Grizzly Encounter, I turned to Steve again for his knowledge and expertise in those fields. He got to know Brutus at a young age, but they had never really developed a true one-on-one relationship. Brutus was three years old at this point and Steve felt that it was time to give it a shot. Brutus weighed 500 pounds and was in his adolescence. This was a good time for Brutus and Steve, as Brutus wasn't too big yet and was eager to form relationships, as any teenager usually is. Steve and I discussed how we would introduce him to Brutus. First I recommended that he sit next to Brutus's indoor kennel in order for them to spend some time getting to know each other without physical contact. Steve sat in a folding camp chair next to Brutus's kennel every night and read a book. It was a great way to take baby steps. But sometimes even with baby steps, it can be one step forward and twenty steps back. I remember coming into the apartment attached to the bear indoor kennel area. Steve was sipping his morning tea and had a funny grin on his face. He began to tell me about his attempt to get to know Brutus. The night before, just like every night that week, Steve went into the kennel area and plopped down in the chair to read. Steve was feeling comfortable with Brutus, so he decided to sit closer and take the relationship up a notch. Steve had read about a chapter when all of a sudden the chair was swiftly removed from underneath him. Brutus wanted the chair inside his kennel, and a tug of war ensued. Steve didn't stand a chance, but he gave it his best shot. As he finished the story we walked back into the kennel area to find the remnants of the chair in Brutus's kennel. Brutus looked like he was folding it into some sort of origami design. I walked into his kennel and removed it from his mischievous paws and told him he was bad. He knew he was bad, as he gave me a pouting look. Then he gave Steve a look that would be the equivalent of sticking his tongue out.

This wasn't a great start to this new relationship. Some more timed passed, and Steve learned to sit further back.

Then one day Steve decided he was ready for an up-close introduction to Brutus. We decided that Brutus and I would go out into the sanctuary with Steve and we would put the relationship to the test. As the three of us exited the handling building with Brutus on a leash, all seemed fine. I could sense a bit of nervousness from Steve, as you would expect. Brutus seemed not to care about Steve's presence, as he had grown comfortable with him by this point. We walked to the top of the hill, I took Brutus off the leash, and the body language exchange began. Brutus walked toward Steve very matter-of-factly but then just walked by him very closely. It was a test. Brutus was giving him a subtle sizing-up and walked abnormally close to Steve to make him react. Instead of holding his ground with authority when Brutus walked by, Steve took a very natural small step back and settled on his feet, the way you would if you thought you might get pushed. In grizzly bear language, this slight motion was a billboard of flashing neon lights saying "I'm submissive!" Brutus made a quick U-turn, pounced on Steve, and sat on him, similar to what a golden retriever would do to a new puppy in the house, to make sure he knew who was top dog. He wasn't being violent, just establishing his place on the totem pole. Brutus just lay there and looked up at me as if to say, "Look at me, Dad, I've got a new toy!" I couldn't let it go on in front of me, so I quickly put the leash on Brutus and removed him from Steve. I will never forget Steve's face as he took a deep breath from his Brutus-squished lungs and said to me, "I have had enough." That was the end of that. Though Steve and Brutus still have a relationship of sorts, I can see in Brutus's eyes when he looks at Steve that he sees a subordinate toy and does not respect him. This is potentially dangerous for Steve, especially now that Brutus weighs half a ton.

Not all relationships have to start off so rocky. I remember the day that Brutus and Jake (another rescue bear) met for the first time at the sanctuary. When you introduce bears to each other, you never know what is going to happen. It is like setting up a blind date. You speculate about how they might get along, but you really don't know until you get them together. It's a very nerveracking situation, because unlike a blind date, if they don't like each other, they will try to kill each other. Breaking up a bear fight is no fun, but it is part of my job if the "date" escalates to that point. In preparation for such a meeting, all possible outcomes are considered, and I take step-by-step precautions. I will often let the bears see each other first, over a fence or through a kennel wall, but no physical contact is allowed. You can get a preliminary idea from this interaction, but it has to be brief, as this enforced separation can be frustrating to the bears, and could cause aggression. We set up a fence for Jake and Brutus and let them out on either side. They ran back and forth anxiously, trying to find a way through to the other side. There was no sign of aggression, just extreme curiosity and playful body language as they stood on their hind legs and pawed the air as if they were waving to each other. Then they would drop down on all fours and swing their heads playfully side to side, a demonstration of utter happiness and excitement. Jake would roll over and do somersaults to demonstrate his submissive intent, and Brutus would leap on top of rocks and bounce up and down, showing his desire to play. I quickly decided that it looked as if a good relationship was about to develop, one that would last a lifetime, and might be the most important relationship of their lives. It was bittersweet. Here was my old wrestling partner, my best friend, meeting a new friend, one that could hold up his end of the bargain better than I could. Don't get me wrong—it was about time Brutus could wrestle with someone his own size. My back and knees had about had it!

When Jake and Brutus came face-to-face, they stood on their hind legs and engaged in a sort of wrestling dance. Friends at first sight! They grappled for hours, until both bears were exhausted. They took turns pinning each other down, and rolled all around the sanctuary. A new bond of companionship had been formed. Now he had two bear best friends, Jake and a female named Sheena, who had been in the sanctuary since the beginning. You would think that Sheena and Jake should be instant friends by default, but that wasn't the case. Whether it was jealousy or they were just not each other's type, when Jake met Sheena, she chased Jake with murderous intent from one end of the sanctuary to the other. Her ears were pinned back to the side of her head, and all of her muscles were rigid, ready to battle. Jake held himself in a very different manner. Fear was painted all over him. You could see terror in his eyes! Jake tucked his short bear tail under his hind end and ran for his life. There was no compassion in Sheena's pursuit, and Jake knew it. Jake dove into his den to escape, and Sheena paced on the outside, waiting for him to come back out. But she would have to wait for another day, as we secured Jake inside and made the decision to wait. Grizzly bears are as individual as humans when it comes to personality, and they also have bad days and good days. With so many personal variables, you just never know what you are going to get. This character variance holds true even in the wild.

As I watched the bears come and go that day up on the mountain, feasting on moths, I couldn't help but think of the journey each of these bears had taken to get where they were, all of the interactions they had had and the miles of Yellowstone country that they had seen. If a person had the experiences that these bears have had, they would be the most interesting human in the world.

We hiked back down to base camp, as long and hard a trek as ascending the mountain. When we reached camp, we gobbled up dinner and then tucked ourselves into our sleeping bags and tried to get some sleep. The next morning was more of the same, a half-awake treacherous climb toward the peak. As we arrived in the feeding area I noticed a sow with two cubs, each about the size of a loaf of bread, and they stumbled and fell as they moved about the rocks. It simply amazed me that they were even here. Their little legs must have already walked hundreds of miles, and now they are climbing in some of the most rugged terrain in the world. No wonder they are such tough creatures. If that wasn't enough danger for the little guys, the mountain was crawling with big male bears who would surely enjoy a cub for dessert. Just then I noticed a big bruin coming closer to them. The wind was blowing strongly away from him, and the mother seemed not to catch his scent. He was getting very close, and finally the sow saw him. She charged down the mountain toward him and then unleashed a blast of paws on him with lightning speed. He backed down a bit, but not enough. She retreated to her cubs and took them up the hill in a sprint. I watched in amazement as the cubs ran full speed up the nearly vertical mountainside, one that I could barely hike up. I knew that grizzly bears were amazing athletes, but to see two tiny cubs cover that much insanely difficult ground in such a short time truly blew my mind. This aspect of the grizzly was something I had never thought about. I watched as they clung to cliff faces, maneuvered up over very steep ice fields, and climbed the unclimbable. I found caves in the most extreme areas that had sign of grizzly bears. The popular idea that these massive bears are clumsy and cumbersome was shattered as I watched these giants maneuver like mountain goats through the rocks and crags. The mother and her cubs outran the male bear and safely disappeared over the ridge top. Humbled by their amazing physical prowess, we shuffled our tired bodies back down to base camp.

After a night of high-altitude insomnia, and an unforgiving, uneven sleeping pad of rock, we slogged up the same treacherous route to revisit the bears and to film more of their behavior. But today we had an idea. We were going to have our support team of the two strong guys from Cody bring our tents, sleeping bags, and dinner to the top in order to avoid another crazy morning trek. The day started off badly for me. After falling on the snow field, I had to emergency self-arrest, a procedure of rolling over on your stomach while sliding and using your ice axe as a brake to stop your momentum from taking you onto the rocks below. This woke me up better than any coffee could, but it scared me all the same. After reaching the summit that morning, the wind seemed to be hurricane force, and dark clouds were building on the horizon. And if the environment on this grizzly-saturated rugged peak wasn't enough, add a lightning storm. Lightning is ultra-dangerous on open exposed terrain like this moth site. People die from lightning strikes regularly in situations like the one we were in. As the storm blew in we scrambled to look for cover. Lightning had already begun to snap on the ridges and peaks surrounding us. With no cover in sight, we found a large impression on the leeward side of the mountain, and assumed an anti–lightning strike position, one that you are taught in standard mountaineering courses. You sit on the heels of your boots and try to balance on your toes. You lace your hands across the back of your head and prop your elbows on your knees for support. As the storm passed over us, we all sat silently waiting to be struck by the next bolt of lightning. When one struck nearby, we would all flinch in fear. Finally the storm passed. We were glad to be out of what seemed like harm's way, forgetting where we were and what other hazards were imminent.

We spent the rest of the afternoon trying to find moths to film. With millions of moths on the mountain, the three of us spent over an hour without finding even one. Without the extremely sensitive nose that a grizzly bear has, it was truly like looking for a needle in a haystack. I was nearly going to give up when I saw one scurry under a rock. I flipped the rock and pinned it down. Finally, a moth! We filmed the moth and I explained its importance to the camera. Then my curiosity and hunger got the best of me. I often find that most of the food items grizzly bears in the Yellowstone region eat are quite tasty. And after eating very little, and being completely sick of eating the same flavor Clif Bars for four days, I decided to give a moth a shot. I tossed it in my mouth and crunched down on the little winged, juicy insect. To my surprise, it was absolutely delicious! It tasted like a honey-roasted peanut. As moths spend the weeks on the mountain, they eat only wildflower nectar, which gives them a very sweet and nutty taste. They are rich in fat and protein, which is why they are so attractive to grizzly bears. After I swallowed the moth, I frantically started to dig for more. If I had known that these moths were like candy, I would have ditched the camera and spent my days on the hillside with the bears. I found seven moths total over the next hour, and devoured each of them. It was hard work, and I likely spent more calories than the moths gave me. My crew watched my bearlike behavior in disbelief, and seemed to be quite entertained, but did not partake of the insect appetizers.

As afternoon came, we began to look for a campsite nearby. We didn't want to be too close, as we didn't want to disturb the bears or have them disturb us in the night. Just finding a flat spot was hard enough, but to find a soft spot was impossible. All that existed was rock and ice. We finally found a nice little flat boulder field on a small saddle. We attempted to pitch our tents in the virtual tornado of wind, a task that took all of us to accomplish. We spent a great deal of time reinforcing our tents and tying them down to boulders to keep them from blowing off the mountain. To our dismay, once we had our tents in place the wind picked up, and so did the bear activity. First it was a sow and three yearlings, who walked within fifty yards of our camp. Then, a solo young bear, and then another. Not only had we picked a wind tunnel for a campsite, it was a grizzly highway! It was too late now to try and find another site, and the last thing we wanted to do was to be caught stumbling around at night on this mountain. We set up a camera to capture a time-lapse of the sun falling behind the peaks, and then scarfed down some cold slop for dinner and took Tylenol PM for dessert to help with the upcoming sleepless night. As I crawled into the tent, the wind took it up a notch. Now the tent fluttered in the wind so badly that I could not hear anything else. I buried my head in my sleeping bag and tried to sleep. If a bear had clawed its way into my tent, I wouldn't have known until he was on top of me. It was horrific, and the thought of sleep seemed impossible. As I lay there thinking of a quiet soft bed at home, I heard a strange sound. A howling sound. I thought it was the wind and disregarded it. I was nearly asleep when I heard the noise again. This time it was more distinctive. It was a voice. I listened more carefully, but the tent flapped like the wings of a hummingbird, drowning out nearly every other sound. Again, I heard a moan, then suddenly the wind died down just enough to clearly hear the words "Hey, bear!" I snapped into action! I grabbed my bear pepper spray and threw on my boots without tying them. I zipped open the tent and emerged into near darkness. A soft glow of the disappearing sun barely lit the horizon. I heard Thomas yell again, "Hey, bear!" I scanned the camp, and when I realized that he wasn't there, I turned on my headlamp and briskly marched toward his voice. Suddenly, standing in front of me was the silhouette of a grizzly. I aimed my headlamp at the bear, who was standing entirely too close for comfort, and right on the fringe of our camp. When my light hit him, his eyes reflected a reddish glow, and we stood there motionless. A bear in the night is often a dangerous one, and one wandering this close to camp was likely up to no good. I couldn't see him well in the low light, so I could not read his or her intentions.

To my left I heard someone clambering over the rocks, and I turned to look. It was Thomas, and as he neared, the bear slowly ambled off out of sight into the dark and windy night. Thomas had gotten to his tent only to realize he had forgotten his camera that was capturing the time lapse. He wandered alone out of camp to retrieve it, but upon his return in the dark, he found a bear investigating the outskirts of our camp. When the bear registered his presence, it did not seem to care, a reaction you'd rather not get from a bear in the night. He attempted to haze the bear away with his exclamations, but the bear stood its ground, and perhaps could hardly hear or smell him in the wind. My arrival on the scene seemed to deter the curious bear just enough. Thomas and I returned to our tents, and I remember lying there and thinking about what I'd just seen. The wind howled, and my mind raced. I bet I only slept an hour that night. And I was lucky to get even that. In the morning, as we packed up our stuff and cached it for the day, we realized that making the 1,500-foot morning hike up the snow field with heavy packs was still a better option than the previous night's ordeal. We captured the most surreal grizzly images I have ever seen on that trip. I experienced grizzly bears as never before. In just five days, we literally lived like the grizzly bears, and I had even eaten like one. Now our bodies were worn out. We were running on empty and wanted to go home. It took every bit of energy to make our way back to civilization. The mountain had whupped us. I remember thinking about those little cubs again as I pushed myself through the fatigue. This was the way they lived every day. They don't have a comfortable option, and their life is constantly unforgiving. They rarely get second chances, and they must endure all that is thrown at them. It is no wonder that the Yellowstone grizzly bear is the toughest animal on earth.

CHAPTER 12

UNBREAKABLE BONDS

W E ARE NOT ALONE ON THIS PLANET. WE ARE NOT THE only ones who exist and feel. We share what it is to be alive with other species of all shapes and sizes. All animals, including humans, perceive the world from their own perspective. The lives we lead are very different, but each moment lived is equally valid.

Yellowstone's Swan Lake Flats is a stunning place—the sounds of waterfowl in the morning, the sun rising over the snowy mountains, the mist and fog, and the playful elk calves. But life is short for some of these beautiful creatures.

Born on a cold, rainy, foggy morning in early June, a

calf is tucked safely away in the sage. Its new life is overwhelming. Its thin fur and skin barely keep it warm as it instinctually lies in a tight ball trying to keep out of sight until its mother returns. Its scentless body is a nice evolutionary trait to keep it safe. The sounds of passing cars and human voices are part of its new audio reception. Although it was born near a road, it has not yet learned to fear them. Sandhill cranes call in the background along with the constant hum of western chorus frogs. The elk calf thinks it hears its mother returning. The calf anxiously awaits its mother's warm milk, but it's not Mom. The drive to stay alive comes from deep within. This young calf has only stood a few times in its life and walked even less, but now its deep instincts tell it to run. It runs and finds it's being followed. It cries in fear and panic. Over and over it calls to its only ally, its mother, whose whereabouts are unknown. Not knowing if its cries are heard or if they would matter, it runs into a lake. Now it starts to swim, something it has never done. But is still being pursued by an animal it knows somehow it must escape. Its little body is running out of energy and it heads back to shore. As the water grows more shallow, the calf's small hooves sink into the muddy lake bottom and it tries to wade to solid ground. Now it has reached the shore but can barely stand because it's so exhausted. For a day, this calf lived in one of the most beautiful places on earth, breathed some of the freshest air, listened to the most beautiful songs of birds and frogs on the planet, and stared at some of the most picturesque mountains in the world. On this day the calf would stand for the last time on the shore of one of the most beautiful lakes in the world, and have its skull and neck crushed by the jaws of a grizzly bear.

After the bear spent an hour eating most of the twenty-five-pound calf's body, the happily full bear ambled off into this same gorgeous place to live another day, but in this brutal land, no one knows who's next. Every moment and breath is special, especially when existence is so tenuous. It's the insecurity and fragility of life in this outstanding wilderness, and the bonds that all creatures share to keep the cycle of life moving forward, that make it special. A bald eagle lands, picks some leftovers off the calf's carcass, and takes off toward its nest where hungry eaglets are waiting.

The bond that is formed between a mother grizzly and her cubs is one of the strongest emotional connections in the animal kingdom, and has fascinated people for centuries. This family arrangement is complex. It consists of not only the cub-to-mother bond, but the sibling tie also. I have witnessed mothers who favor one cub over the others, something that we have all seen in the human world. I have watched as two cubs play joyfully together, while they relegate the third to sit and watch. If the third cub ever tries to interject, it is picked on in tandem by its kin. This also is something that we can relate to. But imagine the beginning of your life as a grizzly cub. You are born into a deep underground lair. It is cool and dark, secure and safe. You are bound closely to your mother and siblings for months, with nothing to worry about, and your universe is limited by the walls of gravel, soil, and roots. Occasionally you hear the moan of a passing blizzard, and catch a scent from some distant unknown source hinting that there is more to your world. After months of isolation, you emerge from your subterranean bubble into a life that is bewildering, yet thrilling and filled with curiosity and danger. The perils and struggles that now are a constant in this new life make the bear family's dependence on each other crucial. I have witnessed it time and time again: a mother bear with two cubs clinging to her hip and each cub clinging to one another as they venture across the unpredictable landscape.

Most cubs stay with their mother until they are two or three years old. Then one day something snaps, and the whole dynamic changes. The bond is shattered in a violent and catastrophic division of the family that is initiated by Mom. The female inflicts a brutal assault on her cubs that is met with panic, confusion, and fearful disarray. I watched this event once, and it was very disturbing. The sow lunged, roared, and devastated the cubs with a whirlwind of bites and swats, and then, in an effort to escape them forever, sprinted away. The cubs followed their mother, bawling and bellowing, and when they came near her, she inflicted another round of punishing assaults. This happened over and over, hour after hour, as the cubs desperately attempted to make their mother reconsider. But to no avail. I often wonder what triggers the mother's decision to leave her cubs behind. Perhaps it's their size and their increasing food requirements. She would have to have grown weary trying to feed not only herself but the cubs. Or is it some sort of hormonal or innate desire to move on and mate again, feeling now that the cubs no longer need her and can fend for themselves? Whatever the reason, the mama bear leaves and doesn't look back. The siblings will lick their wounds together, spend the next few days huddled close together, crying and staring at the world around them in terror. As brutal as this is, this is the way every grizzly bear starts its life.

One cold spring evening, I sat on a barren ridge and hunkered close to the ground among the boulders to escape the wind. I scanned the vast open snow-dusted sagebrush with my binoculars for signs of a grizzly bear. I noticed the mother first as she sprinted across a giant snow field, leaving a cloud of ice crystals in her wake. As she reached the other side, her two cubs desperately tried to catch up, screaming and whining. They tried to run across the deep snow but slipped and fell, their little legs postholed into the deep wet snow. Their mother never even looked back to see where they were. When they finally reached the other side, their mother was now miles away. They sniffed the air and the ground but could not find her trail. There they sat, as the sun fell in the sky, and faced their first night alone.

The next morning my film crew and I came upon the newly orphaned bears. I remembered the bears from the previous year. I had watched them follow their mother as yearlings, learning the way of the land, and digging in the earth for roots and rodents for their first time. At that point they were taking their first leap toward independence and self-sufficiency. Now their mother's teachings were being put to the test. I was surprised at how fast they had begun to rebound. The cubs, which looked like brothers, had already begun foraging for roots through the frosty ground just a day after the breakup. Either their hunger was overriding their loneliness, or else they were just keeping busy and active to keep their minds off it. The brothers were cautious and on the lookout. Half of the time they were attempting to eat, the other half they were on guard, lifting their heads and nosing the air. The biggest danger they would face would come from other, larger male grizzlies, who are extremely territorial and hostile to newcomers. This was their first morning without the protection of Mom, and little did they know how monstrous the day would be.

Earlier that morning I had had an eerie and close encounter with a large, dark grizzly lurking in the shadows of an old growth stand of Douglas fir trees. I had spotted a sow digging on a plateau, and I used the trees as cover to get a closer look. As I edged along the tree line, focused on the sow, I first noticed the crunchy footsteps of a large flat-footed animal walking through the frozen snowdrifts that remained in the shade of the massive trees. My personal cameraman and friend, Rick, now a grizzly-tracking vet after many intense days of filming, caught a glimpse of the bear within twenty yards, but it disappeared into the forest. I felt vulnerable knowing that a big bear was close but invisible to us. I didn't want to retreat and risk stirring the sow, so we stood still and listened for more footsteps. I could hear the crunching of paws and the light woofing sounds of an uncomfortable and agitated bear. We continued to stand motionless. Finally, an escape door opened and the sow moved off and out of sight. We retreated to an open ridge so that we could get a wide-angle view of any approaching danger. That's when I noticed the brothers.

Rick and I situated ourselves in an open meadow, hiding low in the grass, remaining as still as bushes, and keeping the wind in our face. The brothers frantically excavated around us. After we had spent an hour filming the tandem digging and eating, laced with an occasional sibling skirmish, the vibe on the mountain changed. The young bears noticed the trouble first. The wind carried a foreboding scent sharply over the far ridge and straight into their noses. This would be their first time facing adversity on their own. I noted to camera that I could see their concern, and in retrospect acknowledged the likelihood that it could be the same large bear that I had encountered earlier in the timber. Adult male grizzly bears do not like young bears. In fact, they try to kill young bears, and it was likely that the two cubs had faced many a tormenting boar in the past and had been fiercely protected by their mother, but now they would have to defy the boar on their own. My speculation was confirmed as the large male bear crested the horizon. His appearance alone demanded attention and humbled not only the young bears but our entire film crew. As he strutted toward the brothers, they had no interest in standing their ground. Instead, they sprinted right toward us. We held our ground, and continued to document the event. The cubs passed within fifteen yards of us, not giving us a second look. They may have been aware of our presence, but at that moment we were the least of their worries. As they galloped off into the far stand of spruce and firs, the boar now set his sights on three other little bumps in the meadow. We were crouched on sacred digging grounds, where grizzly bears have come for decades for their first meal of spring. This land was rich with food sources, and all less dominant beings were to follow the law of nature and yield to the bigger and badder. We were not bigger or badder, and he was coming straight toward us like a bear on a mission. The wind was blowing in our face, and without our scent, there was no doubt that this big male thought we were more bears that he needed to punish. I turned my back to the approaching bear and addressed the camera, describing the situation I could see over my shoulder in the reflection of the camera's lens. Rick held the camera rock solid, and I watched the mirror image of a massive grizzly closing in. I knew and explained to the camera that I needed to identify myself as a human as soon as possible. The bear had crossed a dangerous line. The distance he had reached now gave us a fifty-fifty chance of either his running away or defending himself and inflicting a good mauling on us. I quickly stood up to show the bear my human outline. He stopped dead in his tracks just nineteen yards away. I waved my arms slightly and said, "Hey, bear," in a nonthreatening monotone. That was enough. He spun around on a dime and sprinted in the opposite direction. This was the decision we really wanted him to make, although scaring bears away is always our last resort. The best part was that it was all captured on film. It was a perfect demonstration that when face-to-face with a grizzly bear, accurately calculated decisions can save your life, and that we can coexist with grizzly bears if we are willing to understand them.

Another winter passed, and the brothers likely once again shared the comforts of their communal den. In a predictable fashion, both the brothers and I returned to the same area to see what the new year would bring. I often see the same bears returning to the same area year after year, those bonds between them still unbreakable, and this year would be no exception. Every bear that I encounter on these sacred feeding grounds was brought here by their mother at a very specific time. The skills that a mother teaches her cubs are essential for their survival. The brother bears were back, but this time they were not side by side. In fact, the first time I saw them they were about a mile apart, foraging in different meadows, moving in opposite directions. My guess was that they traveled here together after emerging from their den, and once they arrived, the desire to be alone kicked in and they were gradually making their break from each other into the life of an individual grizzly bear. Their newfound confidence was still a little riddled with traces of insecurity. But as I watched them return to the area where I had seen them stand beside their mother two years before, it was apparent to me how much is learned in the grizzly world, and how little could be chalked up to just instinct.

In the episode "Expedition Wild: Project Kodiak," I recorded how the behaviors that a mother passes on to her cubs are vital. I went to Kodiak Island, Alaska, to witness mother bears teaching their cubs how to fish for salmon. I was astonished at the variety of fishing techniques. Some females would chase the fish in the shallow water, and then pounce on them. Others would sit on top of waterfalls and wait patiently for the salmon to leap into their waiting mouths. No matter the technique or the place they chose for the fishing hole, all of these skills and details were taught to the cubs; they were not instinctual. I returned to Montana and attempted to teach Brutus the same skills. He had never had the opportunity to learn any skills from his mother, plus she was not a wild bear. Although I built waterfalls and trout ponds, and went through the motions that I watched the females demonstrate to their cubs, I could not replicate the teachings I had witnessed. The perseverance and determination that mother grizzlies have is irreplaceable. Every second of every day is a learning moment for a bear. In its minute-by-minute struggle for survival, it is crucial that during its cubhood a young bear be a good student, otherwise it means certain suffering or even death.

Grizzly bears are very much like humans, with both a rational and an emotional side, and are subject to the same influences we are. I once heard a story of a young bear that had been radio-collared for a study. These collars are fitted with a piece of canvas that will rot off, so that when the bear grows, the collar will not choke it. Most bears are then either refitted or go without a collar for the rest of their life after the collar falls off. This poor bear's collar did not function as planned, and as the bear grew bigger, the collar dug deeper into its neck. The collar never released its grips, and began to imbed itself into the bear's neck. The bear became agitated and grumpy, and could not relieve its pain. It developed an animosity toward humans and began to be very aggressive toward them. One autumn day, the pain was extinguished when a hunter killed the bear with his rifle to keep from being mauled. It was not until this unfortunate event that the source of the bear's agitation was discovered. When you hear the other side of the story, although you never wish injury on a human, you understand why the bear acted the way he did.

CHAPTER 13

THE GOLDEN CHILD

I T'S EARLY JUNE IN THE YELLOWSTONE REGION. THE GRASS is green, the leaves have fully emerged, and summer is almost here. Almost. It's snowing, after all. Cold, wet, and snowing. Little grizzly cubs are five months old at this time and about the size of a loaf of bread. They have spent only a month out of their warm dens, and they have likely walked their first hundred miles. Their tiny feet begin to be callused, in preparation for the thousands of miles they will travel, along rivers, through vast valleys, and over mountain passes. When Brutus was this age he still spent most of his time in the house. He didn't have to worry about snow; he crawled up on the couch, stretched out and snoozed to the hum of *Golden Girls* reruns. His little paws were as soft as a baby's bottom and he walked on carpet and linoleum. His swimming hole was a deep bathtub, his wilderness the lawn of the back yard, and his mountain the steepest flight of stairs. Brutus is a special bear, and he knew it from the start. From the time he was a cub I could see the special gift that Brutus possesses. He has an ability to engage people unlike that of any creature, wild or domesticated, that I have ever seen. Brutus did not learn to walk until weeks after the expected time, because every time someone laid eyes on him, they would have to pick him up, hold him close, and carry him around. He undoubtedly loved the attention. He has always been the roundest, cutest, and fuzziest bear, a real-life teddy bear. Being cute, paired with his funny, charismatic personality, has caused people to fall in love with him over and over again. Brutus is a natural charmer. He was born to be the bridge between the human world and the wild world. He has made this very connection all his life. Brutus not only loves it but is good at it. The idea to have Brutus serve as an ambassador to his wild cousins was not my choice but one that Brutus made. People who see Brutus get excited—he causes them to care. They start to ask questions, wanting to know more about the animal that just swept them off their feet. I answer their questions, while Brutus continues to charm them, encouraging them to learn more. It was so powerful and apparent from the very first encounter—we were changing minds, generating an appreciation, and curing prejudice, one person at a time. This dangerous intoxication often forces people to consider seemingly irrational things. For example, when Brutus and I are on a movie set, the film crew, cast, and my team go through an extensive prefilming safety meeting. One of the first things I say, before anyone even sees Brutus, is that no one can touch, pet, or hug Brutus. This comment is usually met with laughter and comments such as, "Yeah, right, I will want to hug a grizzly bear." In fact at that point most people are scared and are considering leaving. It only takes about five minutes once Brutus walks into the scene before I hear the first person melt and succumb to his magnetism. "He is so cute," they exclaim. "Can I pet him?" "I love you Brutus!" My crew is now on constant watch for what was unthinkable ten minutes earlier. What had been a bloodthirsty beast moments earlier has turned into a soft little teddy bear, completely irresistible to everyone, and it's all the result of the innate gift that Brutus has.

However, despite this wonderful gift, we all must never forget that Brutus is a grizzly bear. We must respect him for what he is. He is special, no doubt, but he is still one of the biggest, most powerful animals on earth. But his power goes much farther than just physical strength. He can change stubborn minds, cure prejudice, and cause people to care, and that is what drives me to continue my work with National Geographic, Montana Grizzly Encounter, and, of course, this book.

BRUTUS WAS BORN AT A WILDLIFE PARK THAT WAS overpopulated. Space was at a premium. Unfortunately, once a bear is born into captivity, it can never be released into the wild. In Brutus's case he had only one option, euthanization, a practice that is legal and common in many such wildlife facilities that need population control. Animals that are privately owned are treated much like livestock when it comes to rules and regulations. To prevent a captive facility from becoming overpopulated, animals can be "surplussed," or removed humanely. I could not let this happen to Brutus. I felt compelled to scoop him up and be his champion.

Brutus did not go immediately from the wildlife park, where I first adopted him, into Montana Grizzly Encounter. In fact, this process took years, during which time Brutus was moved from place to place. He was like a fugitive or a runaway, never knowing where he was going to spend his next night. He had no definitive place to call home, a situation that began simultaneously with his rescue. The night we decided when Brutus would make his break from the wildlife park into his new life was the Fourth of July, Independence Day. How fitting. With the help of the family of my colleague Ami, we constructed a chain-link dog kennel from Wal-Mart in their garage that was going to be his home until we found the next place. We brought Brutus home and I remember unloading him into the kennel with a proud smile on my face as I thought about the new life that lay ahead of us. Our first moment spent together on our own involved my watching him destroy in just one minute the dog kennel that we had spent a couple of days constructing. Now what were we going to do? We had rented a U-Haul truck to bring him over, so I spent the first night with Brutus in the back of the truck, with him screaming at the top of his lungs, jumping on my face, and terrorizing me all through the night. I remember waking to the smell of bear crap, cracking open the door, putting his leash on, and walking him around the yard, having not slept one minute all night. I lay in the sun in the yard with a leash tied around my wrist and fell asleep while Brutus cuddled next to me and took a nap. I knew that keeping a grizzly bear was tough, but now I had no other choice. The next day I called a friend of mine who had a wildlife park near Driggs, Idaho, and asked if I could house Brutus there until I could figure out something better in Montana. He had no problem boarding Brutus there, but it was going to cost me a little bit of money. It was my only choice, so I took Brutus to the park. Poor Brutus spent most of the next couple of weeks in this strange park, in a kennel among various animals, like mountain lions, badgers, lynx, and bobcats, none of which Brutus had ever encountered before. Ami and I would take turns driving to the park daily to feed him and spend a little time with him as I frantically tried to think of other options. I worked out an agreement with Montana Fish, Wildlife & Parks to keep Brutus temporarily at my dad's house, but in order to bring Brutus from Idaho to Montana, where my dad lived, I needed to get a health certificate in the state of Idaho. I had no real way to transport Brutus so I borrowed a friend of a friend's old rusty horse trailer to drive him down to a nearby vet. The horse trailer had large window openings that I was a little worried about Brutus being able to crawl through. At nearly 85 pounds he was quite a fat little boy, so I put some simple barriers of plywood connected with heavy wire over the openings and figured that should do the trick. As I was driving down the Idaho highway toward the vet at 55 miles an hour, I'll never forget the way I felt when I looked in my rearview mirror and there was half a grizzly bear hanging out of that horse trailer I was towing. Luckily for me, the vet was only about a quarter of a mile away. I kept up my speed in hopes that that would be enough of a psychological deterrent to keep him from jumping. As I pulled into the driveway I remember all the big wide eyes looking out of the vet's office. As the trailer slowed down, Brutus leapt from it, landing in the parking lot, and started running around the parked cars. I, too, leapt from the car, chasing him around and finally catching him, calming him down, and putting on his leash. I remember how foolish I felt as I walked toward the door with everybody staring in astonishment as I tried to keep my cool and make it seem as if I had everything under control. This was my first attempt at being my very own business owner and grizzly bear trainer and I had failed miserably thus far. The actual health inspection went very well, thankfully. Brutus awed the vet and the staff by being Mr. Charming, doing somersaults, and making cute bear noises. Now I needed to figure out a way to get him home. I knew there was no way to fix the rusty old horse trailer, so the only option I had was for him to ride in the front seat of the old Dodge pickup truck alongside me. I loaded him in the front seat and walked around to the driver's side. I pointed my finger at him and said, "You'd better stay right there." I wasn't worried. It was only going to be a 60-mile drive, so what could possibly go wrong?

We headed down the highway once again, with Brutus

turning the windshield wipers on and off, changing radio stations every second, and constantly adjusting the volume. I kept readjusting the rearview mirror until Brutus finally bit it off. I was pushing him with my right hand while trying to steer with my left as I screamed at the top of my lungs to try to intimidate him into some sort of submissive state, but to very little avail. Brutus thought he had died and gone to heaven. He got to be with his daddy in a small, confined area and see some of Idaho's most beautiful scenery, all while listening to various radio stations and playing with all the knobs and buttons he could ever wish for. To add insult to injury, he then decided to pee all over the front seat in his glee. An 85-pound grizzly can piss about half a gallon. The last thing I was going to do was stop the car and prolong this already nightmarish trip. I pressed down on the gas and drove as fast as I could while fighting a happy grizzly bear off in the front seat of the truck. I'll never forget a few passing vehicles whose occupants witnessed the whole thing. I wonder what must have gone through their minds as they saw a twenty-something kid and an 85-pound grizzly bear wrestling down some Idaho highway with a half-demolished horse trailer in tow. I remember getting home, absolutely exhausted by the day, and in typical male fashion picking up the phone and calling Ami and saying, "Come get your kid!"

The next day I needed to prepare to take Brutus to my father's house in Montana. The events that had played out up until now had made it very clear that there were two things I needed more than anything: a secure way to transport Brutus, and a place to keep him until the grizzly sanctuary I was planning for was built. I had thumbed through the classifieds looking for horse trailers, cargo trailers, anything that I could modify to keep Brutus in for a short period of time. It was summer and it was hot, so when I saw an ad for a refrigerated trailer I thought it sounded like the perfect way to both transport and house a grizzly bear. For $600, I bought an air-conditioned, two-wheel cargo trailer that a man had used to transport earthworms (of all things!) from Idaho Falls to Boise every week. A friend helped me weld a makeshift cage inside to make sure that there would be no grizzly bears hanging out the side of it while we were going down the highway. Brutus had his very first customized grizzly bear trailer, and I have to admit I was proud. I remember loading him in, turning on his air conditioning, and parading him from one friend's house to another and saying our good-byes as we were about to head north. I said good-bye to Ami, knowing that she would not be far behind, and headed to my dad's house in East Helena, about 250 miles away.

When I arrived at my dad's, I pulled the trailer into a shady spot underneath a large willow tree and went in to take a break from the exhausting week I'd just had. This was Brutus's first time not being around other bears for an extended period, and with constant attention from people. I remember lying on the couch listening to Brutus bellow at the top of his lungs with discontent inside his new trailer. Part of the agreement that I had with Montana Fish, Wildlife & Parks is that I would keep Brutus on the down low. His trailer was parked in the middle of town, and he was doing his best to let the whole state of Montana know that he had arrived. The cry of an 85-pound bear sounds like something between a person being tortured and Chewbacca. I sprang from the couch and ran outside into the trailer to calm him down. I leaned my back against the corner and he lay on my lap and we both fell asleep. Like anyone by himself in an unfamiliar place, he was lonely.

After a couple of days of sleeping—or should I say trying to sleep—in Brutus's trailer with him, I realized that I had to do something. He had separation anxiety and could not be left alone. I couldn't take him on walks all the time, and I definitely could not sleep any more nights in his trailer. Plus, I had a grizzly bear sanctuary to build. It was for Brutus, so he could grow up being a bear, but I needed some time away from him so I could actually get it off the ground.

Finally, I knew what I had to do: find a companion for Brutus in my absence. My dad thought I was crazy, but he went along with it. He drove me down to the local humane society, so that I could find Brutus a new friend, one who could keep him company when I couldn't. I remember walking up and down trying to find just the right lucky dog who would get to spend the rest of his life being the friend of a grizzly bear. There were little yapping dogs, old tired dogs, and every dog in between. None of them seemed right until I came around the corner, and there was a beautiful, young, calm, black Lab giving me the best lonely-puppy dog eyes he could. I remember that when I said, "This is the one," he wagged his tail and I could see his excitement at being released from this dog hell. Oh, if he only knew where he was going. His name was Judd. He really was the perfect little black Lab, probably a year old, almost fully grown, with a mellow, sweet temperament. He walked perfectly on his leash as we left the humane society. We loaded him into the back of my dad's truck and drove to his house. I wanted their introduction to be perfect. I didn't want either of them to feel pressured into this, as it would be the first time either one of them truly got to hang out with the different species, which was already stressful enough. I put Brutus on his leash and had my dad go into the middle of the yard with Judd on his leash. Judd was happy to be free of the kennel. He was bounding around the yard, sniffing the grass, and having a great time. When I put the leash on Brutus he felt much the same way. He had been in the trailer all day and was ready to bound around the yard and play. As I walked closer to my dad and Judd, I remember the moment that Judd and Brutus saw each other. They instantaneously wanted to be as far away as possible from each other and ran to the end of their leashes. We held our ground as they frantically tried to run in opposite directions.

There they sat, staring at each other, snarling, growling, moaning, and yelping. I remember thinking, "Oh, this is going to be interesting." My dad and I took turns walking past each other. We inched closer and closer ever so delicately, trying to get the bear and the dog used to each other. It wasn't working. It quickly became apparent that they wanted nothing to do with each other, and it seemed like my idea was a flop. Yet, the last thing I wanted to do was take this poor dog back to the pound and spend another night sleeping in Brutus's trailer. In my experiments with animals I knew things like this would take time, so I came up with plan B. I walked Brutus back to his trailer and then went and got Judd from my dad. Now I was going to put Judd into the trailer with Brutus and let them work it out themselves.

About five feet from the trailer Judd put on the brakes. He looked at me like I was nuts. I looked at him and said, "I'm sorry." It took all of my might to shove that poor dog into the cage of a grizzly bear. Brutus ran to the opposite corner bawling and growling and Judd hit the ground and went to his own corner snarling and growling. They sat as far apart as was physically possible and stared at each other across the trailer. I sat with them for about an hour as the standoff continued. Soon night came around and I knew they both needed to eat, so I prepared their respective meals. I put the dishes a little bit toward the middle while giving them enough room to eat comfortably, but my hope was to draw them a little bit nearer to each other in the effort to eat. They never moved all night, and when I returned the next morning, they sat in the same corners with their food dishes completely untouched. After maintaining their ground stubbornly for most of the next day, Brutus was the first to eat. His belly overcame his fears and he made the first step. Judd complained, barked, snarled, and growled, but Brutus lapped up the contents of his bowl, ignoring it all in his hunger. A couple of hours later Judd gave in, too, and had his meal.

Sometime around midnight, I was awakened by the eruption of a dog-and-bear fight. I grabbed a flashlight, and ran outside toward the trailer, which was rocking back and forth like there was a mosh pit inside. I swung the door open and screamed "Stop it!" and they scurried to their opposite corners and looked at me in disgust. This pattern repeated itself for a few more days. I would spend the middle of the day trying to play peacekeeper, trying to get them to get to know one another. Neither of them seemed to want to budge. After each fight, it became apparent to me that it wasn't a physical fight as much as it was vocal and verbal, wherein they were trying to show each other who was the top dog or bear. One morning, I woke up and the trailer was eerily quiet. I have to admit that as I approached the trailer I wondered who was dead. I cracked open the door and peeked in. There, in the corner, were two exhausted animals, cuddling one another in surrender. It was truly a beautiful sight, and I let out a deep sigh of relief. After days of holding their ground stubbornly, the two of them had become best friends. They both needed one another; it just took them a long time to figure it out. Surprisingly, Judd had taken the upper hand. During any squabbles, all he would do was bare his teeth and let out a little growl, and Brutus would back down. Judd had this down to a science and wasn't afraid to tell the little grizzly bear to back off. Brutus loved to tackle Judd and nibble on his ears and Judd didn't mind the roughhousing and would nibble on Brutus in return. They would go for walks together, chase each other around, and, just like any typical grizzly and Lab, they both loved to get in the water and swim. Even though some of the problems had been solved, it was still difficult to take care of Brutus and Judd, as I had to focus on the construction of the sanctuary. So I was very excited when Ami, who had given two weeks' notice at the wildlife park, arrived in Montana. I remember looking at Ami, handing her the leashes, and saying, "Take your kids." Not so surprisingly, the next day, I got a phone call from a Montana Fish, Wildlife & Parks official telling me that there had been some grizzly bear cub sightings in town and some very strange roaring noises coming from my dad's house at night. So I needed to look for a more inconspicuous place to keep Brutus.

My grandmother had a cattle ranch in the valley, with a bunkhouse that Ami could stay in, so it seemed the perfect place. That's what Brutus, Judd, and Ami called home for the rest of the summer. The ranch is a great place, with wide-open spaces and irrigation ditches. It was out of sight and out of mind. We created a play area for Brutus, surrounded by a small electric fence. It was situated next to the corrals, so he could be out in the sun and air most of the day. Ami would sit next to the pen and read books to Brutus while I ran around the state trying to get permits and organizing the upcoming construction. My grandmother was very supportive and my aunts, uncles, and cousins loved to come visit Brutus at the ranch. After a few months, however, Montana Fish, Wildlife & Parks called me and told me I had worn out my temporary welcome.

Through a loophole in an old circus law, I knew I didn't have to get a state permit for a while as long as Brutus did not stay in the same state for longer than two weeks. So that's when the Brutuspalooza tour began. It was on poor Ami's shoulders that the duty of circus master fell. First stop, the great state of Texas. Ami had once worked for a guy who lived in Texas. In fact, her first job, at the age of eighteen, came about when she answered an ad in the paper and ran away to join a circus with a dancing bear act. They would drive from one state fair to another. She would dress in a sequined gown, and waltz with a black bear dressed in a tuxedo and top hat. Ami, Judd, and Brutus spent a good deal of time in southeast Texas living in bayou country, running from the law. John, my other business partner and friend, and I worked frantically to try to put together what we could so the two of them could come home. Brutus traveled around the country in his little custom trailer with Ami for the next few months. Ami would call to give me updates and I would send her money by Western Union as much as possible to keep the two of them alive. I finally came up with a more permanent situation. I asked another friend of mine with a game farm if he would keep Brutus temporarily under his permits. Montana Fish, Wildlife & Parks agreed, and Ami and Brutus headed home. This worked out great because Brutus could stay in Montana, Ami could tend to him daily, I could visit him often, and we could continue to build the sanctuary.

John and I drove all over Montana looking for the perfect piece of property. It had to be a place that was easily accessible for the public, but not a place that any kind of wildlife would inhabit. In order to run a sanctuary properly, one needs to make sure that there's a constant flow of cash to keep the animals maintained and healthy. You must run it as a business while always keeping the animals in mind. So we needed to find something along a major highway so people could easily pull on and off, stop in, and leave with a good grizzly bear education. At first glance the plot we found looked like a field of weeds but it was our field of dreams. It was a small piece of land situated on the Bozeman Pass smack dab between Interstate 90 and a train track. This would seem like hell to a wild grizzly bear but it was the perfect piece of paradise for the bears that we were planning on rescuing. There were gorgeous views of the Bridger Mountains, and the air was cool and crisp, just perfect for a grizzly bear. As I found out soon enough, there were thousands of rules and regulations that one must abide by in order to construct a grizzly bear sanctuary. Up until then, I had had plenty of experiences with regulations of wildlife husbandry so it wasn't completely a surprise. But in order to keep grizzlies in the state of Montana, you must build a very fortified facility. The bears must spend the night within an enclosed building every night, and it needs twenty-four-hour, seven-day surveillance and security. What we thought was going to be relatively simple turned into a major project. There was the construction of twelve-foot-high walls with an additional four-foot fortification underground so the bears could not dig their way out, all surrounded by an additional fence with 10,000 volts of electricity running through it. Our little piece of grizzly paradise soon started to look like a prison. John, Ami, a few friends, and I, including Tim, my mother's boyfriend, did most of the construction ourselves. I would spend hours on the phone talking to wildlife officials, getting insurance papers in order, and running a three-yard front-end loader. Ami would run back and forth to Brutus, make her fair share of phone calls, and made sure we were all fed and happy. John did what he could from California, and would come out to Montana and jump on some heavy equipment whenever he got the chance. Tim was a construction worker extraordinaire and would work sixteen hours a day to help build Brutus his new home. As things began to develop we would get a lot of comments about how much like a prison it looked, but we did not care about keeping people happy. We knew Brutus was going to love it and we knew that there were other bears out there that needed to be rescued who would love it too. We worked very hard and did what we could to finish the project with very limited resources. We exhausted ourselves and our bank account for several months. We got plenty of resistance from the neighbors and a little support from others. At a local town hall meeting having to do with the concerns about our sanctuary, I was tarred and feathered by over two hundred people. But I didn't care, and we kept pressing on to make Brutus a new home.

I'll never forget the day when we had all of our t's crossed and our i's dotted, and the Fish, Wildlife & Parks folks came out to give their final inspection. Finally, with both federal and state permits in hand, we took the bear trailer to go get Brutus and bring him home for good. I know I cried the day when Brutus ran around his enclosure for the first time and got to swim in his pond. It was a new beginning, and we had traveled a long road to get there.

Brutus started to get too big for Judd, and after wrestling matches Judd would wind up limping a little. I felt bad for the tough little Labrador. I knew the time had come for them not to play together anymore. Judd had to live like a real dog now, lying at our feet, begging for table scraps. Though Judd would live out the rest of his life at the sanctuary, he would only get to see and smell Brutus from a distance. It was a sad day, but Brutus and Judd were home now. It was time to rescue some other grizzly bears that Brutus could play with, somebody his own size he could pick on. One of our biggest hurdles was trying to have a life while the sanctuary was manned 24/7. We all tried to pull our shifts, but it was daunting. We had finished the animal facility, but the personnel apartment on the inside of the building wasn't quite ready. It was adjacent to the mandatory indoor bear kennels in the enclosed building. Until it was completed, I slept next to Brutus's kennel on a small mattress. We had no bathtub or shower, so I filled his water trough with hot water and would take a sponge bath in it. It was tough living for a while, but all of this was ours, and we were finally free.

For a long time, Montana Grizzly Encounter was generating no income. All of our resources were put into the sanctuary. We all took turns doing what we could and it was wearing on us, but we believed in what we were doing and knew that someday it would all pay off. There were long stretches when none of us left the sanctuary. I can remember one time when I spent over a month without ever leaving the confines of the fence. I got to hang out with my buddy Brutus but it still felt a bit like prison. Tim would go to grocery stores and pick up day-old produce, and meat that had been pulled from butchers' shelves that they would donate to the bears. Times were tough, and I would go through the produce and meat and pick out

Brutus's and my favorites. What grocery stores throw away isn't half bad, and when you make no money it is doubly awesome because it is free. I got really good at making salsa from bruised peppers, cutting the bad parts off avocados, and making beef or chicken stir-fry. The conditions that the tough times created really gave me an opportunity to learn more about myself. Just years earlier I had been invited to work with an animal trainer I had worked with in the past who was starting a new business. I eagerly drove to Idaho to work with him, because I thought he was the best animal trainer in the world and I could learn so much from him. For eight months, in the shadow of the Teton Mountains, I worked day in and day out with several species of animals. I was training the animals and learning a ton from them. I helped my friend build his business, all while living in a tepee without electricity or running water. This is where I learned to survive off food that was donated for animals and where I realized that I could be alone and enjoy just my own company. Next to a campfire every night I would stare into its light and dream of the day that I would have my own place, be able to exercise my own ideas, and do something that I thought was good for the world. I had also just come off a divorce. I had married too early, long before I knew myself. That relationship ended badly, and I needed to find myself again. I learned so much from the animals during this time of growing and healing. In my loneliness I was forced to dig deeper into their souls for companionship, and only in this type of solitude can one force oneself to dig as deep as I did. I did a lot of soul searching in that tepee, and it prepared me for Brutus and the long months of getting Montana Grizzly Encounter up and running.

When you're raising a grizzly bear you can never be heavy-handed. Look on Amazon or Barnes & Noble and you won't find a handbook on how to raise a grizzly bear. Very few people have gotten the opportunity, and nobody's really documented it. It's mostly just trial and error on one big learning curve. Just like a child, if you react physically with them while you're raising them, it is likely that they will grow up and react physically when reprimanding their own children. If you constantly yell, scream, and throw things around your children, they, too, will likely yell, scream, and throw things around. So in raising a grizzly bear you have to keep in mind that there is a chance that one day you'll have a 900-pound eight-year-old who's going to emulate you. Surely Brutus and I have had our share of ups and downs, and there were times when I reacted poorly, just like any father would. He tested my patience and tested my commitment to him, and sometimes I would just lose my temper. I have watched mother grizzlies reprimand their cubs very violently, but they were always very precise about their punishment and the cubs seemed to understand and take the lessons to heart. However, I did not want to create a violent relationship with my cub, so I knew the only way to discipline him was through emotion. Brutus truly cares how I feel about him. He wants me to be pleased with him. If I call him a good boy it makes him very happy and proud, and on the contrary, if I call him a bad boy, he hangs his head, feels sad, and pouts. Brutus listens to the inflection of my voice. He knows how I feel about him depending on how I speak to him. And I have calibrated a good tone of voice that Brutus can easily translate into how I'm feeling. When I work with Brutus I do everything from whispering softly to screaming in elation and sometimes roaring in his ear in disgust. Brutus understands all of these completely. This communication is something that has taken a long time for us to develop. I also have learned to emulate grizzly bear body language and use it along with my vocal communication to reinforce my intentions. For instance, if I'm charging at him standing tall, throwing my arms around, and roaring at the top of my lungs, he knows that I'm not very happy. On the contrary, if I jump around and scream "Good boy!" while clapping my hands and skipping around, he gets excited and happy that I'm happy with him. He throws his head around, stands proud, and demonstrates his inner happiness. At this writing, Brutus is not yet eight years old, and grizzlies don't mature until they're ten. So for me to believe that the raising of Brutus is finished at this point would be foolish. I've heard some people say that one human year equals two and a half bear years. That would mean at age eight, Brutus will be twenty in human years. Most of Brutus's emotional development has been fully realized, and he understands where he fits in the world, for the most part. But now he is becoming a man and his longing for solitude is growing more and more. Thankfully, the days when he challenged me as a father are long past, and we have achieved a mutual understanding of each other. We communicate smoothly and during the time we spend together we rely a lot less on trial and error. Although I'm not perfect, both of us are more forgiving of each others' mistakes. In the beginning there was a lot of roaring, with me lying on top of Brutus, as we rolled around on the ground and I growled in his ear and called him a bad boy. We understand each other now, with the result that we exchange a lot of high fives and I frequently call him a good boy.

During Brutus's stay at the family ranch in Helena, before the sanctuary was built, we went out on one of our daily walks in the field. It was late summer so the grasshoppers were plentiful and Brutus loved to chase and catch them and have a little crunchy snack. He really, really loves the taste of grasshoppers, as do most wild grizzly bears. We were walking along an old irrigation ditch side by side, waiting for grasshoppers to hop up in front of us. When a grasshopper presented itself, Brutus would chase after it. I also like to catch grasshoppers. When I caught one, I would hand it to Brutus to eat. Once, a giant grasshopper suddenly flew up out of the grass directly in front of us and we both went for it at the same time. As I reached down for the grasshopper, Brutus lunged and bit me in the arm, indicating that he did not want to share. I knew this was bad and I knew I needed to react very sternly as a mother grizzly would in the wild. I attacked him, jumping on top of him and pinning him to the ground with all of my weight. He was already a pretty big bear, weighing over 80 pounds, and 80 pounds of grizzly it about as strong as the strongest man on earth. I had my hands full but I could not back down. I roared loudly in his ear, "NO," and I hung on tightly as Brutus roared back defiantly. I felt like a bull rider, and as he desperately tried to escape I continued to barely hang on as I continued the onslaught of verbal abuse. After ten minutes of rolling and crashing through the field, Brutus finally succumbed to me and lay there silently. It had taken every bit of my energy for this one disciplinary moment. I had self-inflicted scrapes and abrasions over my elbows and knees, and I was sweating and out of breath, but we had a common understanding. That was the last time Brutus ever truly sank his teeth into me. He has since given me bluff bites and I have roared back at him. But he already was reacting before I began because he knew he had done something wrong, and thus our father-son relationship continues to evolve.

CHAPTER 14

SHEENA AND CHRISTIE

THE SPIRIT OF THE WILD WEST STILL RUNS FREE TODAY
in the souls of the untamed, though some of these beings
have found themselves locked away, suppressed, and
abused. Like modern-day outlaws, they are misunderstood,
and alone.

When we got the call in Montana we never would have
expected these two little grizzly bear diamonds in the rough.
They were skinny and a little neurotic from their confined
life, but they were still grizzly bears. The bears' current
owners were ill, and the bears needed a home. The only other
option was death. When the USDA Animal Welfare Information Center called and told me of the situation, I was

thrilled, as it was exactly the type of rescue our sanctuary had been founded for. So my buddy Steve, whom I had nicknamed "Silvertip," and I hooked up the trailer, jumped in the truck, and drove the 1,700 miles to bring these bears to their new home. We had no air conditioner, and it was over 90 degrees when we reached Kansas. As the Rescue-mobile pushed across the great plains, our windows were down, our shirts were off, and we were singing Bob Seger songs. We pulled into northeast Texas, which was a part of the country I had never seen before. I was like a little kid when I saw my first armadillo. I still have a childlike curiosity when it comes to animals, and I had to get a closer look. With the truck and trailer pulled over on the side of the highway, I tried to catch it for examination. Silvertip cheered me on from the cab of the truck. I dashed back and forth in the barrow pit as the little creature did its best to avoid capture. And it was successful. It slipped into a culvert that ran under the road and disappeared. I hopped back in the truck a little disappointed but impressed. As daylight came to an end, Texas welcomed us with the light parade of fireflies. We had a rodeo ahead of us tomorrow, as loading grizzly bears into a trailer is no easy task.

It was bayou country. I remember driving the truck with the trailer zigzagging down the two-track dirt road. I knew something strange was going on when we rounded the corner and I saw a small wire cage surrounded by dogs. Inside was a full-grown baboon. The dogs would gather around the chicken wire cage as the baboon picked fleas and ticks off them. They all seemed to be thoroughly enjoying themselves. We slowed down to watch the scene and then moved on around the corner to a small single-wide trailer surrounded by broken-down cars and a lot of junk—your typical redneck backwoods scene. Tucked away back in the trees, in two small cages, were two beautiful little grizzly bears. It astonished me when the owners took us down there to see how small the little females were. You could see that their muscles had atrophied, and their legs had developed strangely from being cramped for eighteen years in small cages.

When I stared through the rusty bars into the amber-colored eyes of Christie and Sheena, they enchanted me. Though I stood outside their 4-by-6-foot cage, their personal awe and magnetism pulled my heart inside with them. I felt their restraint and wanted to cut the tether that anchored their spirit. I know grizzly bears. I have spent my life watching them in the wilderness of the Rocky Mountains. I have watched them run and play through the shadows and the wind of an oncoming savage thunderstorm. They welcomed the change, they embraced and celebrated the approaching tempest. They were alive, and danced in the rains, and felt at one with their universe. Droplets from heaven would cool their bodies and fresh mountain air would gust through their fur, drying them again. The two bears before me had spent all of their eighteen years here, inside the little circus roll cages that were now rotting around them. Sheena's door was bound by a small piece of twine tied loosely in a square knot. These cages were their universe, the only home they had ever known. They sat here, day after day, waiting for their owners to bring them dog food or bread. On a good day, their owners would have people visit and the girls would get to do tricks for Gummi Bears. In the sweltering heat and humidity of eastern Texas, I imagined that they also enjoyed a good spraying-down with a garden hose. Though it was no alpine thunderstorm, it had to be refreshing, but no less sad and unfortunate.

After careful consideration, we came up with a plan to load them into our trailer. This was going to be difficult and dangerous. Moving a grizzly bear from one place to another can be a nightmare. This would take extra attention, and it was an opportunity for me to draw on my years of experience. I have had years of training in animal immobilization and transfer, but this would still be quite a challenge. I had my tranquilizer gun and miles of rope in the truck. I did the safe and logical thing: I laid a generous trail of Gummi Bears from the threshold of their cage to the back of our custom bear trailer. Inside the trailer, waiting for them, was a mountain of Gummi Bears, a dream come true for the girls. With a snip of the twine, the cage door swung open. I could see the confusion and terror in their eyes. Their world had gotten bigger, a lot bigger, and they were not ready for it. After about twenty minutes, I could see a spark of curiosity in Sheena as she reached her paw out into the unknown. This was a giant step on her part, and for that moment she might as well have been Neil Armstrong on the moon. Christie froze from her pacing to watch as Sheena became her hero and pioneered out onto the lunar landscape. That's one small step for a Gummi Bear, one giant leap for the bear sisters. If they'd known where they were going, they would have sprinted to the waiting trailer, but after five hours of one step forward, two steps back, and about a dozen bags of Gummi Bears and our leftover Subway sandwiches for them and a six-pack of Budweiser we had bought for a post-loading celebration for us, the girls were finally secure in the trailer and their bellies were as full as they had ever been. We had a long road ahead of us, and these little grizzly bears were going from the Lone Star State to the Big Sky State. The grizzly girls had spent most of their lives in a hot climate, so this trip was like moving from the equator to the north pole.

As we headed north through Kansas, Silvertip and I really wanted to see a tornado. The skies were dark, and the radio kept announcing a tornado warning, so we were excited. We got a bit lost in the excitement and completely forgot that we had two grizzlies in the back. We were near Salina, and the dust and wind were really whipping across the highway. The clouds were black and ominous on the horizon. We had our eyes glued looking for a funnel cloud like two little boys. Just then, a massive gust ripped a piece of sheet metal off the trailer and I snapped out of it and remembered our original mission. We pulled over, and I retrieved the piece of sheet metal that had torn from the roof of the trailer and reattached it with rope, and we continued on. The weather continued to be hazardous. When we got to Wyoming we were in a blizzard, the highway was a white-out, and we could barely see down the road because the snowflakes were as big as silver dollars. As we drove through them it felt like we were in the starship *Enterprise* going through galaxies. I started getting vertigo and asked Silvertip if he would drive. He took over the steering wheel and I tried to regroup. We pulled over somewhere on the

Crow Indian Reservation, just inside the Montana border, and slept for a few hours after checking on the girls, who were faring nicely despite the dramatic weather. Their inherent grizzly toughness was coming through in their travel savvy. We woke as soon as the sun came over the horizon, and headed back down the highway with me at the wheel. I thought about what the bears in the trailer must have been experiencing. They left hot and sunny Texas, the place they had spent their entire lives, had driven through tornadoes and blizzards, and now it's freezing! As I drove, I was deep in thought, thinking of the future, the girls' new life, and what Brutus would think of them. As I approached a bridge, I saw that it was completely covered in a sheet of ice. It was too late to hit the brakes. The truck and trailer slid sideways at 65 miles per hour, two humans and two grizzly bears headed for a wreck. I nearly lost control, but then the truck grabbed on to some solid pavement and the whole thing straightened out. My heart stopped. What if we had rolled the truck and the grizzlies escaped and were running alongside the Interstate! That's a mess I don't ever want to try to clean up or figure out. Luckily it wasn't the case, but the girls' first couple of days away from home had been quite an adventure already, and by the time the sanctuary came into sight, the four of us were exhausted.

When we arrived at the sanctuary, the snow was about thigh high. We charged through the deep snow in the parking lot to get the trailerload of bears to the handling building. We had designed the bear-handling area, and it is equipped with guillotine doors so they can be opened and shut easily from a safe location. You wouldn't have to put yourself in harm's way when you're unloading grizzly bears. After a 1,700-mile trip you'd have thought the girls would have jumped right out of the trailer. Well, it wasn't going to be that easy. We swung open the trailer doors into their new indoor, climate-controlled kennels. In each of the kennels, a mountain of bear food, something they had never seen, awaited them. Their new accommodations had all the amenities that any bear would love, but the little female grizzly bears wanted nothing to do with it. They held their ground and stood rigidly, peering out of the back of the trailer. After a few hours, we had tried every trick we had up our sleeves to unload them. Then Ami came up with an idea. She thought we should mimic their former owners. It sounded ridiculous, but at this point we had lost our patience and were willing to try anything. So Ami went to one end, with a cigarette in one hand and a beer in the other, and started saying, "C'mon over here, girls," over and over in a Texas accent. Both of their ears perked up! I don't know if Ami hit certain pitches, or whether it was the Texas accent, or even if it sounded familiar at all. But the bears stirred in the trailer and started making their way out. It was just another example of how intelligent grizzly bears are. They weren't going to get out of the trailer for just anyone. So after another fifteen minutes of hearing Ami's best country hillbilly voice, both of the bears were successfully unloaded into their new homes.

Sheena and Christie needed to get used to their indoor facilities first. So they spent a week inside their own kennels to get comfortable and used to their surroundings. After a couple of weeks it would be time for them to go out into their new habitat and become familiar with the rest of their new world. This is a moment that you think any bear would just love. I remember the first time we opened the door to the outside and gave them the opportunity to go into the sanctuary. Neither bear wanted to. They were terrified of the unknown. It took another week before Sheena, the more adventurous of the two, decided just to poke her head out of the door. Immediately outside the door is a hill, and in order to really see around it, you must climb the little hill. When she reached the top, it's hard to imagine the flood of emotion Sheena was feeling. When she stood on top of that hill for the first time she could see ten miles in every direction. She was now in Big Sky country, and it overwhelmed her. It was the difference between night and day from her old home in the bayous of Texas. Sheena and Christie did the same thing individually the day they decided to explore their new habitat. Here were two bears who never swam in water, never got to dig in the dirt, never ran or even got to stand up on their hind legs. And what it must've felt like for them to have grass underneath their paws, that air through their fur, and the sun on their shoulders after eighteen years of incarceration is something I can barely imagine. They were as close to being wild bears that day as they had ever been in their entire lives. I loved watching them as they got into the pond for the first time and began to swim. There was joy in their eyes; they were playful at last. They were full of a new energy and began to sprint all around the enclosure. They started to wrestle and play. They would dig a hole and then they would play themselves to exhaustion. They were born-again cubs!

Now for the next milestone. Sheena and Christie had spent their whole lives together, just the two of them. It was time to meet Brutus. Sheena got to meet him first. Any time you introduce grizzly bears to one another, there is always the potential of a bloodbath. So in preparation, I grabbed a can of bear pepper spray, a fire extinguisher, and a bag of marshmallows, and stood by as they met each other for the first time. With my fingers crossed, I cringed when Brutus walked out the back door and sprinted to the crest of the hill. Sheena stood on the ridge top and they locked eyes for the first time. They sprinted toward each other, and I feared the worst. At the last second, they reared up. I thought it was the beginning of a bear brawl, but they melted into each other and embraced in a giant bear hug. I gave a massive sigh of relief, gathered my gear, and sat back and enjoyed the show. They were buddies from the beginning, and continue to be friends to this day.

Christie and Brutus hit it off quite well, too, though the introduction of Brutus changed the dynamic. The girls gradually started to form animosity for one another. Call it jealousy, or whatever, but I guess the gals didn't want to share their new boyfriend. Sheena and Christie both had gained a new friend, and their relationship as sisters gradually dissolved into hatred, which surprised me. I really never could understand why. I guess there is some sort of communication through the development of relationships between bears that just isn't obvious to the onlooker. It is another example of the grizzly bears' depth and the various range of emotions that they feel, as nuanced as human behavior, and Lord knows, no one can ever get a true bead on it.

Brutus gained two good friends, both very different, and he treated them differently and was treated differently by them. Sheena is more of a tomboy and likes to play rough. She will very aggressively give and receive during a wrestling match, and if it gets too rough, there are no hard feelings. Christie, on the other hand, was quite the lady, and would not tolerate being treated badly by Brutus. Play never got too rough, or she just quit and ignored Brutus. He hates to be ignored, and would much rather play nice than to withstand a week-long grudge that Christie could inflict. All of this variable interaction that Brutus is faced with makes him a well-rounded bear. In that sense, he is no different from an acculturated human. This aspect, coupled with the various relationships he has with humans, makes Brutus's perception very different from most grizzly bears. With this experience, he has developed patience, compassion, and other virtues that are easily visible in his character and his interaction with humans and other bears.

During the writing of this book, we lost Christie to leukemia. We gave her the best few years of her life, and she gave us her spirit and tenacity, which has driven us to continue our mission. She was a big part of our life and she made her imprint on both the humans and the bears alike, and everyone she touched as an ambassador. We are all better for knowing her. Rest in peace, little lady.

CHAPTER 15

FELLOW HUNTER-GATHERER

W E HUMANS WERE ONCE HUNTER-GATHERERS, WANDERING through vast expanses, foraging for berries, nuts, and plants. Most of the meat we ate was not killed by us, but scavenged. We traveled great distances in desperate search of sustenance, in order to continue life to the next day. It was a constant struggle, a day-to-day battle that rarely showed mercy. Our forward-facing eyes, and teeth designed to eat meat, hint that we were killers, too. We would stalk great beasts instinctually, and bring them down with techniques, tools, and patience. As time passed, we adapted to different needs and conditions and became more efficient, but we are still predators. As Brutus and I stare into each other's eyes, I realize that we are almost the same in so many ways. We eat the same things, desire the same conditions, and long for security and comfort. Long past for my species are the days of picking nuts and chewing on rotten carcasses. Now we can find all the food we want in the security of our climate-controlled homes, inside the refrigerator or on a McDonald's 99-cent value menu, but it does us no good to forget our hunter-gatherer roots. We must respect the struggle that our fellow hunter-gatherers, with whom we share the earth, face every minute of every day.

The Yellowstone grizzly lives in a rugged, semi-arid desert, a wholly unforgiving landscape. America is a land that was once abundant with an array of wildlife, and now there are only a few isolated pockets left, such as Yellowstone National Park. The grizzlies of this landscape are not blessed with the many salmon runs of Alaska, or the 90 percent edible vegetation of the Kodiak Island bears. The Yellowstone grizzly has to walk great distances, cross high mountain passes, and weave through dry landscapes of sage and cactus to find food. Most of their food consists of roots, pine nuts, and insects. They also graze on grasses and plants, which are scattered here and there and are increasingly few and far between. Once in a while, on a lucky day, a bear will find a carcass, and will spend several days picking the bones clean. Other days are wasted wandering, looking for their next meal. The conditions that these rugged little bruins have endured have transformed them into a unique subspecies of grizzly bear. The effects are not only physical but psychological. Some of the direct results of this hardship are their small compact stature and irritable disposition.

When Lewis and Clark headed west, the first grizzly they encountered was somewhere in the flatlands of North Dakota. This was far away from the forests and the mountains. The fruit of the land was the millions of bison, pronghorn, and elk herds. Wolf packs killed grass eaters constantly, and rivers claimed victims from the megaherds as they attempted to cross the raging waters, and the weak or unlucky would drown. The landscape was littered with protein for the grizzlies of that era. Now, the herds have thinned, and the grizzlies that once roamed the plains have moved on to little pockets of wilderness that are still able to sustain them.

When an animal is faced with danger, it has the automatic response of either fight or flight. The nonarboreal grizzly didn't have the trees to hide in like its forest-dwelling cousin the black bear, and more often than not chose to eliminate the threat by giving it a good butt-kicking rather than running away. I have found that grizzly bears usually have a personal "bubble of tolerance," and this bubble will change depending on an individual bear's personality and its current mood, just like people. Bears are no different, and each has its own interpretation and reaction to each given situation. When a human interacts with bears, each circumstance has to be carefully analyzed. I have found that a safe distance to keep back from a bear is 200 yards, but even at greater distances than that, most bears will still choose to run away rather than risk being injured. On the other hand, an unhappy bear having a bad day can charge from over 300 yards away. This is scary because by the time you actually see the bear, it's already on its way to inflict some pain. And at 38 miles an hour, you have only seconds to make a decision, one that needs to be precise and effective. The Lewis and Clark expedition faced many of these types of encounters. They often riddled the bear with musket balls, then desperately reloaded because the extremely tough grizzly, though looking like swiss cheese, was still coming at them fast. After the second barrage of lead, the beast would finally die, giving the entire party of men an adrenaline rush they didn't want. These were the moments that were sensationalized in folklore, and the beginning of the monster was born. If they had only known that they could stop an 800-pound grizzly's rage just by calling him a "bad boy." Emotion can move mountains.

Animals and humans can build bridges to each other, thus giving the human world and the natural world a chance to see eye to eye so that we humans can fulfill the responsibility to be the voices of those who have none.

Despite my own rewarding relationship with Brutus, I by no means advocate people having grizzly bears as pets. In fact, that is the very mess we are cleaning up with our rescue and educational mission at Montana Grizzly Encounter. In my opinion, and in good sense, no one should ever approach a bear whether it's captive or wild. Two of the bears were brought to our sanctuary as a result of people hoping to make "pets" of grizzlies and realizing that it was a bad idea. The responsibility of giving a bear a good captive life costs millions of dollars and is a lifelong commitment. In a perfect world, there would be no bears in captivity and every bear could live peacefully in the wild where they belong. Unfortunately that isn't the case, and so it is the responsibility of the Montana Grizzly Encounter team to give these souls the best life they can possibly have, given their preexisting circumstances.

My relationship with Brutus is extremely atypical, and has come about from years of experience and training. And Brutus is an exceptional bear. Brutus's life is about 90 percent bear. He runs, swims, and digs with the four other bears in the sanctuary. But Brutus loves the other 10 percent human part of his life, too. We don't make him do it, he wants to. It's his extracurricular activity, and he enjoys the stimulus. It's not only our responsibility to keep him physically healthy, but mentally healthy, and this includes his "human" activities, among which is being part of the National Geographic television shows. Brutus gets excited when we pull his trailer up. He knows he is going somewhere and that he is going to have an unique experience that will leave him stimulated and fulfilled. It's comparable to a dog when it sees you grabs its leash. It gets excited and jumps all around in anticipation of its walk. When Brutus's trailer rolls up, he, too, gets very excited. He now gets to do what he does best, which is charm others and be adored. With his excitement and my passion for education, we touch the world and create a bridge between the wild and civilization. Through this bond, it is my hope that someday all grizzly bears will constitute a healthy population in the wild, where they belong.

My relationship with Brutus has been similar to that between your typical father and son. As my career advances, the time I can spend with Brutus has diminished greatly. But Brutus is not a dog or a human. Brutus is a grizzly bear.

People ask me constantly if, after being away from each other for weeks or months, he will remember me or try to kill me. As ridiculous as it is to me to hear that question, it is one I address on a regular basis. The thing is, a bear is a solitary creature. A dog or a human is much more gregarious, and somehow we want to project these characteristics onto other species. A bear spends its first three years with its mother. The mother-cub bond is a strong one, but when it's time, it's time, and life alone begins for the cub. Any congregation after that is the direct result of sex or food. Mating season will couple bears for a few weeks, or massive food sources, such as a salmon run, will make bears come together, but even at that, they always maintain their very own personal space. This does not mean that bears automatically forget all of their past relationships. As I mentioned, bears have amazing social memories, and many relationships continue to evolve over a lifetime. Brutus is becoming a man now. Long past are the days of needing people for emotional support. He likes human interaction here and there, but in small doses. I notice he is enjoying his "bear time" more and more, but that in and of itself is not hard for me, or any other human, to relate to or understand. Most friends of mine cringe when their parents or in-laws come to spend more than a week with them. They find themselves uncomfortable after a while and, reminded of the days when they had to rely on adults, they long for their independence once more. Most people don't like to be told to do anything, or to have to follow other people's rules or standards. Brutus feels the same way. When I come around, he deals with my rules and standards for the sake of seeing Dad, just like we do with our parents. But after a short time, Brutus just assumes that I pack my bags and head back where I came from. I respect him for what he is. It is my obligation. I need to let my boy grow up. Sometimes it hurts my feelings a bit, but emotion aside, I know its best for him. Some folks misunderstand this "lack of time" as neglect. This criticism comes from the same people who dress their dogs in human clothes, anthropomorphism at its most ridiculous. My job as a dad now is to make sure that our mission to educate the world about grizzly bears moves forward, and that Brutus is happy in his life as a *bear*. Producing television shows, writing books, and giving presentations are the best way I can contribute my skills. I often reflect back on the times when Brutus needed me more, and like any parent, I wish I had done some things differently. Then I realize that the remorseful "shoulda, coulda, woulda" is foolish, because look at him now: there's not a more perfect bear in the world! No matter how he was raised, and what mistakes we made, he is better for it, and so are the lives of the grizzlies that my team and I have rescued over the years.

We have both turned out all right. It's interesting that we started turning into men at the same time. Brutus is greatly responsible for turning me into a man, and in many ways he has made me who I am now. Over his lifetime, he has made me accountable for all that I do. He made me realize my dreams. He inspired me to be ambitious and to push forward no matter the obstacle. He has always been my reason and motivation. Through Brutus, my life has more purpose and value. I am the only human that can stand safely beside him, the result of mutual trust and love. The proof shines in the connection. I am the superman dad now. My presence usually means some kind of adventure or experience for Brutus. He looks forward to these adventures, and it's apparent in his excitement when Dad walks in the door, as he throws his head back, pricks up his ears, and eagerly awaits the next experience.

The trust that Brutus feels for me was demonstrated one day when he was about four years old. It was the first day of principal photography for the feature film *Iron Ridge*. After a couple of hour-long road trips that included a forty-five-minute stop to change a flat tire on Brutus's trailer, we wound our way up a small mountain road to the location of the day's filming session. As my crew and I prepared the site for Brutus, we checked in great detail for any hazards or pitfalls that might be contained within the bear zone to prevent any danger. With all the wiring, posts, cameras, and lighting in place, it was time to bring out the bear. We had quite an ambitious shot list that day, so we had to be efficient. After running through various shots, including Brutus chasing an actor with a piece of salmon tied around his ankle by a shoelace, we moved to a small stream location for one of the final shots of the day. Brutus needed to walk through some dense brush, come out to a mark in the creek, and do a fake growl and swat the water. As he came through the dense brush, I noticed him struggling a bit to get through. I figured there must've been some rose bushes whose prickly thorns were causing him some discomfort. I encouraged him to continue but I saw that he was having an unusually tough time. I stopped the shot and went over to see what was the matter. As I approached him he made direct eye contact with me and held himself in a very humiliating way. The look in his eyes not only showed embarrassment but desperation. When I reached him, my heart sank. A long strand of rusty barbed wire had remained hidden in the brush when we prepared the set, and Brutus had managed to get tangled in it. It was digging into him and must have been incredibly painful. Most animals react to situations of pain and confinement with a fight or flight response. There have been several occassions when I've approached an injured animal, and even though we were friends, they had lashed out at me in desperate pain. When I carefully got closer to Brutus to assess the situation, I noticed how precarious it was. He had tangled his testicles in the barbed wire, and as a fellow male, I sympathized with him on an extreme level. I tried to comfort him by saying, "It will be okay, buddy." I hesitated in my own selfish fear to dive right into the situation, but when I looked into his eyes again I could see that he wanted my help, and I couldn't let my friend down. I placed my hand on his side and rubbed his fur to let him know I cared. He continued to look me in the eyes and held very still. As I attempted to untangle him from his nightmarish ties, he gently lifted his leg to aid in my rescue attempt. It was amazing that he trusted me to such a degree. If I had been in his situation, I don't know whether I would've trusted anyone to do the job; I would scarcely have trusted myself. It was a very intricate and delicate process with a lot at stake, and it reminded me of trying to defuse a time bomb. All the years as a kid playing the board game "Operation" had not prepared me for this task. Hair by hair, I unwound

Brutus from his confines. He continued to hold unbelievably still, never losing eye contact. He had trust written all over his face. I remember everybody on set—the bear crew and the film crew—holding their breath, watching anxiously. As I unraveled the last of the rusty barbed wire, Brutus looked me in the face as he stepped forward, free from his captor. Everyone on set sighed with relief as if I had just saved the world. I'm sure in Brutus's mind, I had.

CHAPTER 16
BRUTUS THE SHOWMAN

G RIZZLY BEARS HAVE PERSONALITIES AND CHARACTERS as varied as humans. Some have short tempers and some are laid-back, some are shy loners and others are hams. I have watched this unfold countless times in the wilderness. Like the first day on any job, people always are checking everyone out. Who's cute, who's smart, who's tough. And like humans, when bears come together, they must figure out a temporary hierarchy as well. We did this on the playground, in high school, and at the office Christmas party. The same cast of characters exists in a grizzly congregation. There is the shy bear, the bully, the class clown. And when we humans encounter them in the wild, the reactions can be relatively predictable if you know who you are dealing with. You don't want to be too passive with the bully, but try not to be too hard on the shy guy. So where does Brutus fit in the world of the grizzly? He is the coolest, most laid-back, charismatic, charming, intelligent, handsome man around, and he knows it. He definitely has an ego, something people would argue only we humans have. During a live interview with Oprah Winfrey via Skype, I answered Oprah's questions while Brutus was busy trying to get the most camera time. No kidding!! He nudged me out of the way every time I tried to speak, and crowded the camera. The more the audience laughed and cheered, the more he reacted to this auditory stimulus. Brutus tossed his head around, gave me kisses, and wiggled with joy.

He has expressed this characteristic many times. He always plays the crowd and knows he's good at it. At the premiere of *Iron Ridge*, we were supposed to do an onstage demonstration in front of 1,800 visitors before the screening. We practiced what we were going to do over and over and got the routine down pat. But when you added the ingredient of the large audience everything changed. One might expect the roar of a large crowd to be intimidating. Not for Brutus. When the curtain rose and Brutus heard and saw the crowd erupt, he quickly improvised, went into show-off mode completely disregarding what we had practiced. He stood on his hind legs, getting an instant roar from the crowd. Then he waved his paws as if he were batting at butterflies, causing even more of a ruckus. He flung his head around in elation from all the attention. The crowd just ate it up, and so did Brutus. You could see his

TOP: *A grizzly waits to snag leaping salmon out of the air.* BOTTOM: *Sharing is not in the grizzly way.* FOLLOWING PAGE: *Casey and Brutus spend a sunny spring day together in Montana.*

OPPOSITE: *Casey glasses for grizzly bears hunting for elk calves in Yellowstone.* ABOVE: *Casey and his wife Missi in Kodiak, Alaska.*

Best friends for life.

TOP: *Casey teaches Brutus to fish just like his father did.* BOTTOM: *On set filming* Expedition Wild: Project Kodiak.

Casey trains Brutus to "pseudo snarl" for treats.

Jake and Maggie wrestle in the snow at the sanctuary.

TOP: *Late fall in Northern Yellowstone Country.* BOTTOM: *Casey looks for wildlife along the Yellowstone River.*

Views while trekking the Yellowstone Backcountry in late fall.

ABOVE: *Casey makes dinner during the filming of* Expedition Wild: Yellowstone Winter. OPPOSITE: *Casey stands on the sacred "digging grounds."*

ABOVE: *Warming up with some hot coffee.* OPPOSITE: *Casey climbs basalt cliffs to get closer to bighorn sheep.*

As gentle as a flower, Brutus is one of a kind.

eyes shining, and it almost seemed as if he was about to crack a smile.

Brutus has stood in front of crowds all his life. Over time, he has figured out that the more animated he is, the more everyone will ooh and ahh over him. It is simple conditioning. He does a somersault, everyone laughs, so then he does more, and the crowd goes wild. I have even watched him recognize a camera, especially a large professional television camera. When one is anywhere in his vicinity, he will position himself in front of it and start to show off. It makes sense, because over the years, every time a camera was present, I got him in front of it, petted him, fed him treats, and gave him a lot of extra attention. So now, whenever he sees a camera, he goes into "actor" mode. In fact, one of the biggest struggles now is if a producer just wants Brutus to act like a typical bear. When the camera is present, it's hard for Brutus to do anything other than entertain. He has become a celebrity, and he feeds on the attention the same way a person does. He attracts attention because of his personality, and then relishes it. These moments are evidence of a complex soul, and they point up his very humanlike qualities. But it is these very qualities that some people have abused in other circumstances. Circuses and other animal acts often take advantage of an animal's will to please and its desire for attention, and instead of respecting the animal, they use these emotions to exploit it and to make a living. I find it rewarding to let Brutus discover the joy of interacting on his own terms. I like to let him explore himself from the inside, and I take pleasure in watching his personal development based on his own interpretation of his experiences.

This complexity of personality and emotion is evidence of a being of great depth of feeling and intelligence. Brutus is an exceptional grizzly bear, but even in those bears that have a "shy" disposition, I would speculate that it is this very inner depth that makes even the wild grizzly bear such a charismatic creature, and worth every ounce of effort and sacrifice to protect.

I recently gained a remarkable bit of insight from Brutus. If something is physically possible, then he does it. During a recent episode of *Expedition Wild*, we set up a challenge to test a grizzly bear's strength. After weighing a boulder in at a ton, we used a tractor to lift it to place a piece of salmon under it. As soon as Brutus caught the scent of the salmon, he walked over to the boulder, and in one swift move he pushed the boulder to the side and happily devoured the salmon. Then it dawned on me as I stood next to my friend. He doesn't worry much. He is not handicapped by his mind or swirling doubts. If his body isn't capable of doing something, then that is his only limitation. He does not sit there and contemplate, or make excuses, he just does all he can to the best of his abilities. He wanted to move the boulder; it was big and would take a lot of effort, but he could do it, so he did. How wonderful it would be if we could all live that way.

CHAPTER 17

BLOOD BROTHERS

I N THE BEGINNING, MONTANA GRIZZLY ENCOUNTER DID NOT have the means to support itself. So during its construction, we looked for ways to make money. One day I got a phone call from Ken Rowe, a dear friend I had worked with in the past. Ken is a wildlife sculptor who uses live captive animals as reference models for some of his pieces. Ken asked if I knew of any live mountain lion models that he could use. He was also interested in making a promotional video about his work and wondered whether my crew and I would be interested in helping him film and produce the video. It was a perfect opportunity to help out a friend and make some money at the same time. I called my business

partner, John, who had plenty of promotional video production experience, and Troy, a guy I used to work for who
had a mountain lion at his own wildlife facility that I hoped
would remember me and let me work with it.

Troy had rescued Simba six years earlier from Arizona
where his mother had been shot by a hunter, leaving her
cubs orphaned. When I first saw Simba and his sister they
were no bigger than squirrels, two helpless little creatures
crawling around in a basket filled with white towels,
chirping like birds begging for something or someone to fill
their bellies. They did not know where their mother was,
and had now traveled thousands of miles from Arizona to
Montana, passed from one truck to another in a relay of
wildlife officials, headed north away from the desert to their
final home in Montana. I picked up little Simba and tried
to get him to suck on a baby bottle for the first time. He
dug his claws into my arm and in his confusion bit at the
nipple, not knowing what to do with it. That wasn't the last
time he used my arm as a pin cushion.

As business picked up and Simba grew up on the wildlife
farm, he became one of the animals we used for film and
photography. He was active and athletic and loved to sprint
and jump, so he made for intense television sequences.
With all of his untamed spirit and spunk came its share of
wild and dangerous moments. In the years I worked closely
with Simba I had several eye-opening moments in which he
showed me that he was still very much a wild animal inside.

One of those moments was the day we were hired to do
a documentary about mountain lions and a producer
wanted us to have Simba chase, take down, kill, and eat

some captive pheasants he had brought along. This seemed simple, and we were sure Simba would be happy to do it. So we loaded him in the truck and drove him to a nearby ranch to film the sequence.

A decade ago it was not uncommon for a documentary to use a combination of captive and wild animals in the production. Then some well-known wildlife television producers were caught staging a captive mountain lion killing a captive bighorn sheep. After that incident, there was a purist movement in wildlife filmmaking, and even though the staged acts were completely legal, no network or outlet would touch your production unless it was done ethically. But before that, anything was fair game for good TV. Predator/prey setups happened almost every week at the place I used to work, whether it was filming wolves on a carcass and then introducing a wolverine for a massive battle; letting otters swim and catch trout in a man-made pond; or having a Canadian lynx chase snowshoe hares through the snow, surrounded by fence.

So this day was no different from any other, and it seemed simple. We had the ingredients, Simba and a small dog kennel full of pheasant not knowing what was about to happen to them. In fact, as we pulled the birds out one by one and threw them into the meadow, they must have thought they were being let go. But unfortunately for them, from his kennel in the back of the pickup truck, Simba would lock in on his target and anxiously await the opening of the door. With the word "action," the producer would press the Record button on the camera, the door would swing open on Simba's kennel, and in one leap he would be running toward a confused pheasant. The pheasant would give Simba a little run for his money, but as Simba closed in, the bird would take to the sky and attempt to escape. Simba, with his Michael Jordanesque leaping ability, would jump fifeen to twenty feet straight in the air and hook the pheasant with his claws and bring it back to the ground with a crunch of his jaws. The first couple of pheasant were killed quickly and devoured by Simba with no problem. Now we had only a few left, and the picky producer wanted Simba to eat them in a more picturesque setting. That's when the "fun part" of my job kicked in!

Now we'd let the pheasant go, with the cameraman ready, and open the door to Simba's kennel. The athletic cat would sprint, jump, and then make the kill. But now that Simba had the kill, the producer wanted us to take the pheasant away from him and put it in an area that was more suitable for his composition. As my wrangler partner, Shane, and I approached Simba, he would hunker down and snarl and growl. He did not want to give away the quarry that he had just snatched from the sky. Shane and I had done this thousands of times before with other aggressive animals, but never with Simba. We had a game plan. Like two wolves sneaking up on a bear feeding at a carcass, we came at him from opposite directions and tried to distract him from the pheasant. This was not met without a violent defending of his kill. A lot of the captive animals would easily have submitted to us, for they thought we were the boss. Not this cat. He was full of fighting spirit, and we were going to have to earn our pheasant, as he viewed us as equals. Simba's best defense was an offense, and he dropped the pheasant and came at me to change my mind about wanting to take the pheasant away. Whenever Simba lunged toward me, Shane would step in and fend him off. This action would turn the assault toward him. Then I would step in and lure Simba away from Shane and turn the assault toward me. This went on over and over and over again until Simba became tired of the back-and-forth and ran back to his kennel, leaving the pheasant behind. Not an easy way to make a living and definitely not the safest way. We were young rookies in the animal world, we enjoyed the adrenaline rush, and even though it was very unethical and cruel in retrospect, I learned a lot from those days about animal behavior and the do's and don'ts of working with wildlife, namely respecting an animal for what it *is*. Engaging with wild animals without understanding their behavior can be dangerous.

I have a deep scar in the meat of my right hand, just below my pinky, from Simba. Back at the farm, in our daily feeding regimen, Simba had a 1-foot-by-1-foot hole cut in the front of the door to his kennel just big enough to throw whole plucked chickens through. Simba was very much a food-focused animal, so the chickens would rarely hit the ground. He would snatch them out of the air the way he did the pheasant. Day after day, I would get familiar with each animal's feeding habits, and I developed my own patterns for feeding them. As I walked toward Simba, he would usually be in his shelter box and would focus on me as I walked up, knowing he was about to be fed. That day, I grabbed the first chicken and threw it through the hole, knowing that he was going to grab it as usual and start eating it immediately. As I lackadaisically threw the first chicken through, I left my right hand dangling through the hole in the door as I reached with my left hand to grab the next chicken in the bucket. Somehow Simba missed the first chicken and in his mind, the second chicken was hanging there for him through the hole in the door, dripping in chicken blood and grease. I remember the sharp pain when he leapt up and sank one of his claws deep into my hand, pulling it toward his mouth to take a bite. I pulled as hard as I could to avoid the canines popping through my hand. I was arm wrestling with a 110-pound mountain lion, and he had the upper hand, literally. As I attempted to pull my hand from inside the cage, I felt the muscle tear as he pulled in the opposite direction. Finally, with a quick snap, Simba released my hand with a growl, wanting his chicken back. I dropped the bucket and rushed inside with blood gushing out of my hand. Cat claws and mouths are laden with dangerous bacteria, so I knew that I needed to clean it immediately. You can't imagine how excruciating it was to take hydrogen peroxide and a toothbrush and scrub deeply into the deep tear in my hand, already sensitive and throbbing. I scrubbed it clean, stitched myself up, and topped the stitches off with my favorite fixative material, SuperGlue. Compared to all the professional wound mending I have had over the years, I have to say this home job healed up pretty nicely.

So after all these incidents with Simba, you would've thought he'd be the last cat on earth that I would've suggested using to help out my friend Ken. But I had tunnel vision, and Grizzly Encounter needed money. So it was a risk worth taking, and one that I was excited about just because I wanted to be reunited with Simba, who still fascinated me.

So after talking to John and Troy and making arrangements, I called Ken back and said we would gladly make his promotional video in Montana. We scheduled a date, arranged a meeting, and we all drove to a rocky cliff area that was a perfect mountain lion habitat. It was a beautiful morning and everybody was excited to work with Simba. Simba paced anxiously in his trailer as I sat everybody down in the sun and gave them a safety briefing about our photo shoot that day. I knew Simba's history, and I knew mountain lions well, and they are not the most predictable creatures. That morning, my lecture was very detailed and matter-of-fact. Everybody listened attentively, and I could tell that they were a bit nervous.

But once upon the cliff edge, it was just like old times. I could tell that Simba remembered me, and we instantly started to play as if we had never missed a day. I scratched his neck and behind his ears and he purred loudly. Simba lay on the sandstone boulders and posed for photos, and then Ken sculpted in clay as Simba sat proudly like the king of the mountain. Next up were some action shots. I let Simba off his leash and ran up the hill calling to him, and he chased me around the sagebrush. It was a great workout for both of us. The day was going perfectly and the two-hour film session was now coming to an end. I could sense everybody letting their guard down a bit, as if Simba had gone from being a dangerous mountain lion to a big pussycat. Even I had let my guard down a little and was standing there laughing, rubbing Simba on the head and having a conversation with John as he stood behind the camera. I don't know what alerted me, some sort of sixth sense, but I looked down at Simba as his purring abruptly came to an end. A very familiar sight awaited me: dilated eyes and ears pinned down flat. This was not a good situation at all. At that moment, Simba leapt for my throat. In a fraction of a second, I had grabbed him by his throat to fend off the death bite. With my hands around his neck, he dug his claws into my torso and began to pull and move his jaws in closer to my throat. As in any moment of crisis, time slowed to a virtual stop, and for that moment there was only Simba and me.

At the edge of a cliff we now danced the dance of death, looking into each others eyes, as Simba dug his claws deeper into my flesh, pulling himself closer and closer to my neck. I pushed and resisted as hard as I could. And I was not winning. Most would have panicked, but with my years of facing attacks, I knew that the only thing that would save me was focus and decisive action. I knew I was losing and that soon he would sink his canines into my carotid artery and jugular vein, killing me in minutes. I was fighting for my life.

Simba then went to his next killer strategy, picking his hind legs off the ground in a effort to rake his rear claws simultaneously through my stomach wall. Once his feet left the ground, he lost leverage and our dance turned into a spiraling collapse toward the rocky ground. As I continued to look him in the eyes and push him away, we came down to the earth with a giant thud. With the impact, I saw a change in his eyes. Now I had the edge and it was time to take advantage of it. Simba's mind-set went from thoughts of killing to confusion. Luckily, his leash was lying in the dirt next to our bodies. I quickly grabbed the leash, fastened it to his collar, and started to walk him as if nothing had happened. My intention was to reassert control and keep his mind away from attacking me again. I had to walk him a quarter of a mile down to his trailer, and I kept my pace and my control until I loaded him into the trailer. Once the trailer door was latched, I suddenly felt the pain. I knew that during the attack on the hill, he was inflicting damage, but when you're in that kind of situation you never feel it. Now I felt it. I walked back up the hill to help carry the remaining camera gear down, and I was met halfway by Ami and the rest of the crew, who looked like they had just seen a ghost. Ami asked how I was doing, and we pulled up my sleeves to see the damage. It didn't take me long to realize I needed to go to the hospital. We loaded up the gear and I instructed Ami to drive Simba back to the ranch and leave him in the trailer until I got back. John and I jumped in another truck and headed to the nearest hospital, which was forty-five minutes away. I remember telling John to slow down as we were sliding around corners on the dirt road, and telling him that I would not die from the wounds but that I would certainly die from his crazy driving.

We reached the hospital in Livingston, and in typical documentary filmmaking fashion I posed for some pre-stitch photos in the parking lot before we went inside. I told the triage nurse I'd been attacked by a barn cat, knowing that the truth would provoke newspaper and television interviews that I had no interest in giving. She didn't like my explanation but seemed to go along with it. The doctor who examined me thought I had driven a motorcycle through a barbed-wire fence. Deeply concerned about possible infection from the bacteria of Simba's claws, I admitted that I had been attacked by a mountain lion but asked that it be kept quiet, and they agreed. After being stitched up, I headed back to the game farm to face my attacker and unload him from the trailer to his kennel. I spent some time with him, scratching his neck and making him purr. I patted him on the head and left him behind for the very last time. Now it was time to find anything useful from the attack that I could. I wanted to sit down with my crew and go over what had happened and how we could've avoided it, and analyze how we had handled an emergency situation.

I had no idea what anybody else did or didn't do during the attack, so I let them tell me, one by one, their side of the story. I remember in the middle of the attack saying the words "Spray him" in a very low-key way. Part of our emergency plan was the use of bear pepper spray on a attacking animal, and I knew that no spray had been deployed even when I asked for it. I found that most of my crew had been confused or frozen, or made bad decisions. I also learned that Ken, who wasn't supposed to do anything, had tried to reach between Simba and me to grab my bear spray, but was unsuccessful. It was a great learning moment for all of us, one from which I wear the scars proudly, because I know that my crew will react differently next time. There's no better way to learn than from an experience of such intensity. Sometimes it takes an actual emergency to know exactly how you will react.

That evening we finished off the film shoot with Brutus and a little baby mountain lion cub that was the exact same size as Simba when I first met him. I remember Brutus sniffing my bandages and wondering what had happened to me. He sympathized with me and was very gentle, never tearing at my bandages or being extra pushy. He knew that his friend was hurt and gave me the compassion that I deserved. I could tell by his actions and body language that he could feel that I was in pain and that something was wrong. He moved around me slowly, and poked his nose gently at me in sympathy, looking at me with his loving brown eyes.

When you sign up for your animal body language class, it comes with its share of "learning things the hard way" assignments. Animals never lie; they will lay it all out there for you. With Simba, I had created a cat-and-mouse situation, and he held up his end of the bargain. I should have been smarter than that, but when we make mistakes, we usually pay the price. Whether the moment is violent or gentle, an animal's honesty is constant. This is what makes it easier to understand the actions of animals than those of people. Humans possess the capacity to deceive, which makes us unpredictable.

Simba taught me the power of wild emotion and passion, and it helped me understand the unconditional love Brutus has in his heart. He appreciates every moment I spend with him because he lives only in that moment. I have the responsibility to make sure that Brutus's life is full and happy, to understand his wants and needs, and to make sure that he isn't pushed to the point of having to defend himself. Wild animals are just that—wild. Forgetting that can leave a deep wound or even cost you your life. I reflect every day on my scars and how I got them. That reflection fuels the reverence and respect I hold for Brutus.

CHAPTER **18**

BEARANOIA

W E HAVE TURNED THE GRIZZLY BEAR, WHO WANDERS THE mountains alone, into an outlaw. We fear him in the valleys below. When he comes to town it almost certainly means trouble. The WANTED posters make headlines, and so he vanishes into the forest again, yet still we fear him. He's a solitary soul and means no harm. But when we make mistakes, he seizes the opportunity. He's wanted dead or alive, but he is tough to catch. He is the last of the wild west.

We have been trained to fear the grizzly bear. Every time you hear about a grizzly bear it's because it has done something wrong. One of the grizzly bear's biggest enemies is its reputation. When you read about a grizzly in the newspaper, it's because it has broken into a family's cabin looking for food, or a female protects her cubs, as a good mother should, and leaves some poor guy with a couple of hundred stitches. When you see a grizzly in a movie, it is always part of some bloodthirsty nightmare, which is good for Hollywood but far from the truth about bears. Unfortunately, most people make their judgments base on this representation. They believe that grizzly bears want to kill and eat people. And every once in a while it happens, but people are vastly more likely to be struck by lightning, or hit in the head by a falling coconut. When most people go into grizzly country, they go with fear. Growing up in Montana, I found that the majority of the locals feel the same way or even though most of them have only seen a grizzly from a mile away or through a spotting scope, or else they have seen a brown-colored black bear that has been embellished into a bigger-than-life grizzly. There is a remnant fear passed on from the oldtimers. Most of Montana was settled by cattle ranchers and men looking for gold at the turn of the last century. When the gold ran out, ranching was the only way to make money. Predators were no longer welcome. To lose a cow to a wolf or a bear was devastating in those days. It could be the difference between feeding your family or not. If there was even a small chance that a bear would chow down on some farmer's cow, it wasn't a risk worth taking. Complete eradication was the only way to make sure nothing would happen. And people did their best. Hunting, trapping, poisoning, and setting bounties on all predators was the answer. Most of the wolves and grizzly in Montana were killed off in this fashion. As generations passed, the bears' reputation as a cattle and man killing machine was handed down through stories and ideals. Even today, some of my most savvy Montana mountain men friends are terrified of the grizzly. They say things like "if it got that close to me, I would have shot it," or "I'm not hiking up there, grizzlies are all over that place."

Every year one or more bears die just because of this mentality. I read the stories in the paper, and I listen to the accounts of the mauling victims on the local news, and I recognize over and over again that either the attack could have been avoided completely or that something could have been done to prevent the loss of the bear's life. One example is the use of firearms in self-defense of a bear attack, or should I say bear encounter. Over and over again, regardless of what the statistics show, people feel safe behind their guns when they go into the wilderness. But over and over again, you read about a wounded or dead bear, and a guy with his face torn off. The fact is that in most of those cases, the face was torn off *after* the bear had been shot. Doesn't seem too effective to me. They just don't want to eat us. It has happened very few times in very unique situations, usually a starving and desperate bear combined with an injured or ill-prepared human.

This morning I read the latest grizzly bear news on Google. A man hunting pheasant north of Choteau, Montana, was walking through some thick brush. The area had a lot of buffaloberry and the grizzly bears usually gorge themselves there in the fall to fatten up for the winter. In the interview the hunter gave, it was quite apparent that the presence of a grizzly bear in the area was a surprise to him. If he had done his homework, he would have known that the area was frequented by grizzlies. Unfortunately, he shot and killed a female bear and left her three little cubs to die. The loss of four grizzly bears of this ecosystem and population is fatal. Whenever I read stories like this in the newspaper, it reinforces the need for public education about grizzly bears. These bears died as a result of ignorance. If the hunter had been carrying bear spray in addition to a shotgun, all four bears would still be alive. But he went into the area without taking the proper precautions, which include learning about the animals that live in the area as well as being prepared for a possible encounter. He is still alive, and we're all thankful for that, but unfortunately the protective mother bear and her defenseless cubs lost their lives. I have read the exact same story countless times. "The bear was going to eat him" is a common phrase, and one that's far from the truth. But this is what the public believes, and you cannot blame them because they've all been Hollywoodized. All the sensationalized films about the bloodthirsty grizzly bear who stalks people through the woods feed the frenzy. As children we snuggle with teddy bears, but at the same time we watch TV and films that show bears destroying humans with their claws and teeth. The result is people walking through grizzly country who are confused about the creature that they share the area with.

The Boy Scout motto Be Prepared is about much more than bringing the right equipment into the woods. It also means having accurate knowledge and awareness of the animals that share them with you. You don't need to be a grizzly bear behavior expert to be safe in a grizzly bear habitat. We are the adaptive species. We can carry bear spray, put up electric fences, or carry our food in bear-proof containers. There is literature all over the Internet teaching you what to do and what not to do while you are in bear country. Four dead bears is four too many. With the increasing effects of climate change, urban sprawl, and other factors that the bears are already facing, the introduction of ignorant humans into their habitat is very detrimental. It's wonderful that grizzly bears are in our wilderness, and we need to ensure their continued survival in these areas.

CHAPTER **19**

THE HUMAN SKUNK

T HERE IS A WAY TO DEFLECT A BEAR AWAY FROM YOU IN any situation, and that is bear pepper spray. I have yet to read about someone who has used bear spray during an attack and has been killed, and the injuries of those who were mauled are less extensive, and once the spray was deployed, the bear disappeared immediately. If it is a sow, she will pass the spray experience along to future bear generations. A dead bear does not have this opportunity. I like to make the analogy with a skunk when I am explaining it to children, but it works for adults, too. When you see a skunk, you avoid it at all costs because you have been sprayed or someone has told you about the results of being sprayed.

Being sprayed by a skunk or by bear pepper spray is a miserable experience. Grizzlies are smart creatures and they will come to the same conclusion. The next time they see humans, they will avoid us at all costs, the way we do when we see a skunk. And so goes the game of coexistence. We are the adaptive species, so we have to make the adjustments. These are the adaptations that will save our wild places and, in turn, that will save us.

People kill bears with rifles all the time despite the overwhelming evidence that it is not a good idea. Big bears are hunted every year in Alaska and killed with one shot, but these bears are usually unaware of their hunter, eating on a hillside or walking over the tundra. When you have a bear charging you at 35 miles per hour, and you have to make a kill shot, you have to be Jesse James, the famous gunslinger, known for his accuracy and swift hand. But every year, firearms are carried into grizzly country. This deadly combination of ignorance and power results in lost lives. What happens in most cases is that the bear is wounded and not killed. This causes the bear to increase its fight response. So instead of the warning slap that you were about to receive, you get a barrage of claws, consequences of the bear's painful anger. I like to use another analogy when putting the two choices, bear spray and bullets, next to one another.

A police officer is called to the scene of a bank robbery. As he approaches the building, his adrenaline runs high and he is on edge. Suddenly, an intense firefight breaks out between the robbers and the police. He fires back, takes cover, and fights for his life. The moment is so intense and all of his body's defense mechanisms are operating at such a heightened level that when the battle is over, he doesn't realize that he has been shot in the arm. Now do you think a grizzly bear, reacting to a threat, hopped up on the same personal defense chemicals pumping through its blood, will notice when it's been shot? In fact, unless you can place that bullet in a very small vital area, the bear won't even flinch. The same thing happens when police use pepper spray on crazed men high on methamphetamine. But modern society refuses to give up guns and continues to wound bears. Men get themselves mauled, and it's the bears who get blamed.

The battle to get the grizzly bear off the endangered species list is going to have to be fought on all fronts. It is going to take the effort of fish and game departments, environmental groups, and especially the public.

Recently, there was an educational project that needed some funding and support. The project was an educational kiosk that would be placed along the highway near the east entrance of Yellowstone. This is a highway that sees a lot of visitors, most of them people who live or are traveling in grizzly country. The importance of educating these people in the do's and don'ts of being in bear country is absolutely essential to the bears' survival. The kiosk's producers went to many sources to drum up minimal finances to make this a reality. Even more important, they wanted to get it done by summer so it would have the greatest impact due to the high volume of vacation traffic. Unfortunately, they ran into some major speed bumps. But not speed bumps of logic, as you might think, but more of the kind you might find on the kindergarten playground. One agency would not allow the show to go on because they found out that an environmental group had contributed money to the cause. This project had no environmental twists or agency rhetoric, it was just a factual infomercial of sorts that would save both grizzly bear and human lives. It was put to a halt because of the "I won't be your friend if you are friends with them" political mentality. Some things never change, and ladies and gentlemen, these are your tax dollars at work. That year eighty grizzly bears died in the Yellowstone region.

THE SOUL OF A BEAR

I T WAS NOT TOO LONG AGO THAT HUMANS WERE PLAGUED by some very irrational thoughts and ideals. Females and people of certain colors were not considered the equal of others. Over time, these prejudices have abated to an extent and their ridiculous nature has become more apparent. All of the universe is made of the same protoplasm. We are all a collective universe of individual energies. Pain is felt in the same way from one being to the next. Emotion is not exclusively ours. It runs deep in the lives of all living things, but in these times, many of us choose to ignore this immutable truth. We must respect these characteristics that all beings possess. As we dig deeper into the makeup of their souls, we find that we are not all that different, and that the basic foundation is the same. Love is love.

I held Brutus in my arms when he was about the size of a loaf of bread. He looked up at me and stared into my eyes as I bottle-fed him. We were the same, just two beings in this universe, experiencing mutual love. Sharing the moment, breathing the same air, we were both filled with an overwhelming feeling of elation. Then all of a sudden, tears formed in his little brown eyes as he continued to look at me. Simultaneously, my eyes began to flood with evidence of a mutual emotion. Several years later, Brutus was lying in a large hole that he had dug in the shade at the sanctuary. I could tell he wasn't feeling well. He was lethargic and lay on his side almost motionless. I walked over to my buddy and soothed him with soft baby talk, saying, "You will be okay, Brutie." He gave me a small glance and laid his head down with a big sigh. I sat next to him and gently rubbed his belly. He hugged me with one of his massive paws and pulled me closer. There we sat. I was now in his powerful arms, rubbing his belly. He had a terrible tummyache and needed a friend and some comfort. We locked eyes and began to cry together. This struck me so deeply that in that moment the whole world changed. If this giant grizzly bear can feel this way, then why not every other being in the world? From that moment on, I never looked at anything on earth the same way. It was the greatest gift I have ever received, and it came from my friend Brutus.

We have been hiding behind the flames of our campfires for centuries afraid of the unknown that lurked in the darkness outside of the firelight. There we sat safely and told embellished stories of the horrific monsters and beasts that waited for us in the shadows. Fear of the unknown seems foolish. Some of us are pioneers and explorers, seeking to understand the unknown. Others cower from the obscure world. Like outer space, the grizzly bear's soul is an undiscovered wilderness that we gaze at in awe and in fear. We guess and contemplate what it might hold and are afraid of the possibilities. But until someone reaches deep into the vast unknown and learns what lies there, it is only theory and speculation. We have climbed the highest peaks and explored the bottoms of the oceans, but there is one frontier on earth left to explore. It is the souls of the beings that we share this planet with. We cannot understand and protect something we are afraid of, and a grizzly bear is one of the most misunderstood animals on earth. Through my experiences with Brutus, it is my hope that everyone will see the grizzly bear in a different light, and fall in love with all life, inspiring people to care for and protect the planet. The only grizzly bear expert on earth is the grizzly bear, and still I explore the grizzly and hope it continues to give me the gift of glimpses into its soul and its very existence.

CPSIA information can be obtained at www.ICGtesting.com
Printed in the USA
BVIW12n0837121015
421102BV00001B/1

* 9 7 8 1 6 0 5 9 8 2 5 3 3 *